HOME COOKIN'
WITH DAVE'S MOM

HOME COOKIN'
WITH DAVE'S MOM
BY DAVE'S MOM, DOROTHY

WITH JESS CAGLE

PHOTOGRAPHS BY CHRISTOPHER LITTLE

FOREWORD BY DAVID LETTERMAN

POCKET BOOKS

NEW YORK • LONDON • TORONTO • SYDNEY • TOKYO • SINGAPORE

POCKET BOOKS, a division of Simon & Schuster Inc.
1230 Avenue of the Americas, New York, NY 10020

ISBN: 0-671-00060-8

First Pocket Books hardcover printing May 1996

10 9 8 7 6 5 4 3 2 1

POCKET and colophon are registered trademarks of Simon &
Schuster Inc.

Interior design by Elizabeth Van Itallie

Printed in the U.S.A.

I dedicate this book to my
grandchildren: Bryn, Bill, Annagrace, and Liam.
Let this be my legacy to you.

All cooks are debtors
to history, either gone by or
in the making.

PETER VAN RENSSELAER LIVINGSTON

Preparing a roadside
picnic during a family
vacation in the early
1950s.

CONTENTS

Gretchen, 7, and David, 15, dressed for Easter Sunday in front of our home. I made Gretchen's little yellow spring coat myself.

ACKNOWLEDGMENTS

First, I want to thank my son, David, for making this cookbook possible. If I weren't his mom, I would never have been asked to write it in the first place. Thanks to my daughters, Jan and Gretchen, for supporting me in this effort, and to my husband, Hans, who has been my rock, for good-naturedly putting up with the disruption and confusion, for acting as my "go-fer," and for generally always being there for me.

I must express my sincere gratitude to Laurie Diamond, Beth Ann Holden, Caissie St. Onge, and all of *The Late Show with David Letterman* staff members who so generously shared their time and their recipes. Special thanks to Sue Carswell, senior editor at Pocket Books, for her faith (even though her vegetarian tendencies prevented her from trying most of my dishes), and to Craig Hillman, her bright and tireless assistant. Thanks to Pocket Books publisher Gina Centrello, associate publisher Kara Welsh, executive art director Paolo Pepe, and to the rest of the Pocket team

for all their hard work in bringing this together so quickly, namely: Donna O'Neill, Donna Ruvituso, Molly Allen, Sheila Browne, Brian Blatz, Amy Durgan, Liz Hartman, Lynda Castillo, and Irene Yuss. I want to thank Jess Cagle, my talented collaborator, who put my words into a semblance of order, and Gail Eisenberg, who spent so many hours on the phone gathering information. Thanks to Christopher Little, who shot all of this book's original photography with his expert eye, to Beth Iogha, my lightning-quick recipe consultant, and to Elizabeth Van Itallie, for her wonderful interior design.

Thanks to Morton Janklow and Anne Sibbald of Janklow & Nesbit Associates, and to all the inns, bed-and-breakfasts, and hotels that enthusiastically shared their recipes with me for this book. Last but not least, I thank my extended family and friends for their patience, encouragement, and love, and—more to the point—their recipes.

Family photos on the refrigerator. That's P.K. (Pretty Kitty), my beloved cat, in the middle.

FOREWORD

Below are some fond recollections of my mom's home cooking:

I. FAT ON PIE

When I was a young boy, Mom devoted no less than fourteen hours a day to the baking of pies. The benefactors of her hard work were myself and my only friend in the world: a large, sweaty man named Fat Lou. Fat Lou was a high-spirited fellow who spent his life at busy intersections waving at cars. Lou surely loved his pie. Sadly, I lost track of Lou when I checked into the old gray-bar hotel (misunderstanding about a permit for cheerleading camp). But I will always credit Mom's tireless pie baking for the blossoming of that unlikely, yet magical, friendship.

II. THE MEAT-THERMOMETER INCIDENT

During the late '70s, our front yard turned into a veritable refugee camp for Eastern European farmhands. A maze of wobbly card tables was a mealtime haven for foreigners, with their mud-caked boots and amusingly common table manners. Sure, they glistened with the acrid, oily smell of benzene residue, but boy did they love Mom's meat loaf, of which she baked thirty-two pounds daily in one of our home's many ovens.

> **HUMOROUS ASIDE:** One day, for about ten minutes, our entire household was up in arms, screaming and yelling, because we thought one of the foreigners had stolen our meat thermometer.
> It turned out it was just in the dishwasher. We were going to apologize about the frisking, but then we figured, oh, who cares!

III. PRISON

Mom's cookies are great. Simply the best. Once, years ago, during my state-funded vacation, I was able to trade a tin of Mom's cookies for several cartons of Lucky Strike cigarettes. Her cookies are that good! True story!

IV. MISSING TIGHTS

Surprisingly, Mom's cooking even had a direct impact on professional wrestling. It was during my brief career as ring boy for the World Wrestling Federation that Mom developed her now-famous Iron Claw Coleslaw.

To this day, Mom is still a hero to the puffy men in trunks and tights. I, on the other hand, was fired from my pretty sweet job when they caught me swiping Q-Tips and Vaseline. The power of a few jealous, insecure people can be truly frightening.

V. BREAKFAST MEATS

Truck stops (little more than toxic waste dumps, if you ask me) within a fifty-mile radius of our home eventually shut down, due to the success and volume of Mom's cooking. It's a well-known fact that truckers love nitrates, so Mom served them nothing but breakfast meats (bacon, liver sausage links, veal patties, and, as a nod to our neighbors up north, Canadian bacon).

At mealtime, there was the usual grumbling about Mom's refusal to wear a hair net. Responding lightheartedly to criticism, she'd scream, "Get off your high horse, the grub's free, ain't it?"

HUMOROUS ASIDE: When I was in college, I invited my roommate to come and spend Christmas at Mom's house. Boy, did we crack up every time Mom would say, "More fudge, Jethro?" I still get a good laugh on that one.

VI. SMART GUY

The governor was always faking up some big statewide emergency so the National Guard could swing by our house on taco night (Thursday). I intentionally use the word "swing" to make light of how difficult it is to maneuver a formation of tanks in a residential area. But seriously, I salute the patriotic young people who made it over on taco night, week in, week out. God bless you all.

VII. WE'RE ALL WORRIED ABOUT YOU

Well, dear reader, there you have it, my recollections of Mom's home cooking. My only hope is that my thoughtful words have touched the very core of your existence, and that you will remember them the next time you're in a store and are about to shoplift an item you don't really need. Thank you, good night, bon appétit!

—*Dave Letterman, as told to World Health Organization Lieutenant Secretary of Nutrition Jill A. Davis.*

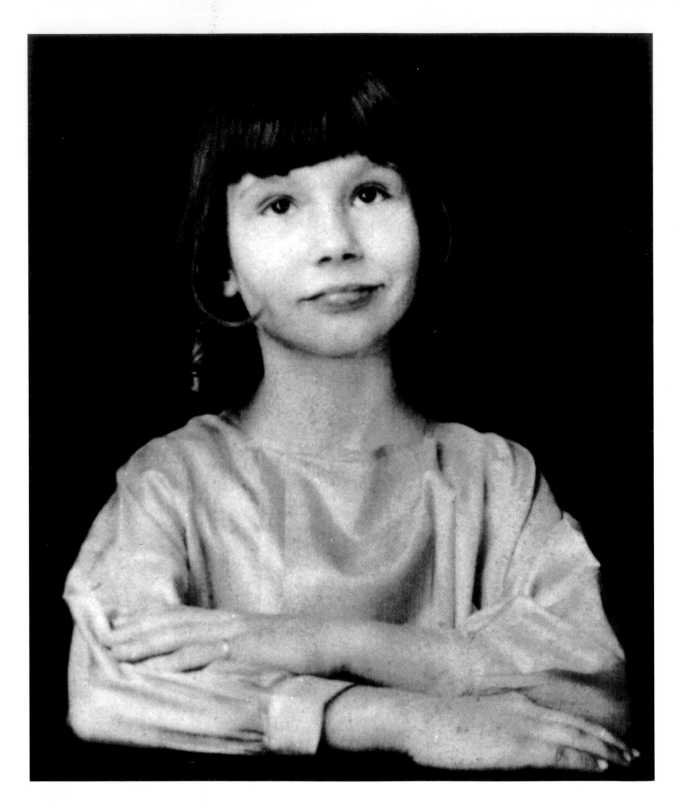

INTRODUCTION

Here I am writing a cook-book, two years after I met the entire world.

In February 1994, my son, the host of *The Late Show with David Letterman*, introduced me to his audience as I appeared via satellite standing next to a ski jump in Lillehammer, Norway. It was cold! And it was a long, long way from Indianapolis, the city I have called home for most of my life. I was in Lillehammer to cover the Winter Olympics for David's show. After he introduced me that first night, a tape of an interview that I had done with First Lady Hillary Clinton—my first interview ever—was aired. Talk about being tossed in the swimming pool and told to sink or swim! At the request of David, I asked Mrs. Clinton if there was any-thing that she or her husband could do about the speed limit in Connecticut, where David has received more speeding citations than he cares (and I care) to count. "Does he have a lead foot?" Mrs. Clinton asked. "So does my husband! What is it about some of these guys with heavy feet?"

During my two weeks in Lillehammer, I had the opportunity to interview Olympic athletes from figure skater Nancy Kerrigan to speed skater Dan Jansen. I presented a canned ham to skier Tommy Moe, fifteen pounds of Jarlsberg cheese to speed skater Bonnie Blair, and a "Dave" button to Gen. Norman Schwarzkopf.

After those two weeks, my life would never be the same. I have made several more appearances on *The Late Show* and

FAR LEFT: **Me, age 8, in a school photo taken in 1929. I didn't like it at the time. Now I think it's kind of neat.** LEFT: **In Lillehammer, cozying up to the Coca-Cola bear.**

viewers seem to like them very much. Here in
Indianapolis, people now recognize me and stop
me in restaurants and shops to tell me how much
they enjoy my son on TV. I say, "Yes, he's very
special, isn't he?" and I mean it.

People now tell me that I'm the only person on
the show who can rattle David. I don't think I
can rattle him. I think he worries that I'm going
to louse up and embarrass myself, which is a very
legitimate concern. But so far, so good.

Before Lillehammer, I had been on David's
show a few times, but only by phone. The call I

The house in the Broad Ripple area where Joe and I raised our three children.

you from the show this afternoon?" she asked. This wasn't an unusual question because David would occasionally call me from the show and we'd talk. I told her we'd find a phone. That afternoon we stopped at a rest stop, but the trucks passing by on the highway made it too noisy for the phone call to be aired on TV. Next we tried calling from a McDonald's, but the phone was in the parking lot. Again, too much noise. Across the highway was a Comfort Inn. We walked in and asked the desk clerk if we could place a call to New York from the lobby phone and then receive a call back from there. She wasn't too sure about this. Hans offered to rent a room for an hour. That request raised an eyebrow.

Finally, she agreed to take my calling card and place the call for me. Maria explained the situation to her, and ultimately everything went off as scheduled. I spoke to David on the air and the woman at the desk got some *Late Night with David Letterman* T-shirts for her trouble. After that, David occasionally would call to ask me about the weather in Indianapolis. Another time he called simply to ask how I made the fried baloney sandwich that he remembered so fondly growing up.

But when I returned from Lillehammer, suddenly I was a famous face. I've tried to use the

remember most came in 1990, when he still had his show on NBC. My husband, Hans, and I were on vacation in Seattle and just as we were leaving our hotel the phone rang. It was Maria Pope, one of David's producers.

"Will you be someplace where David can call

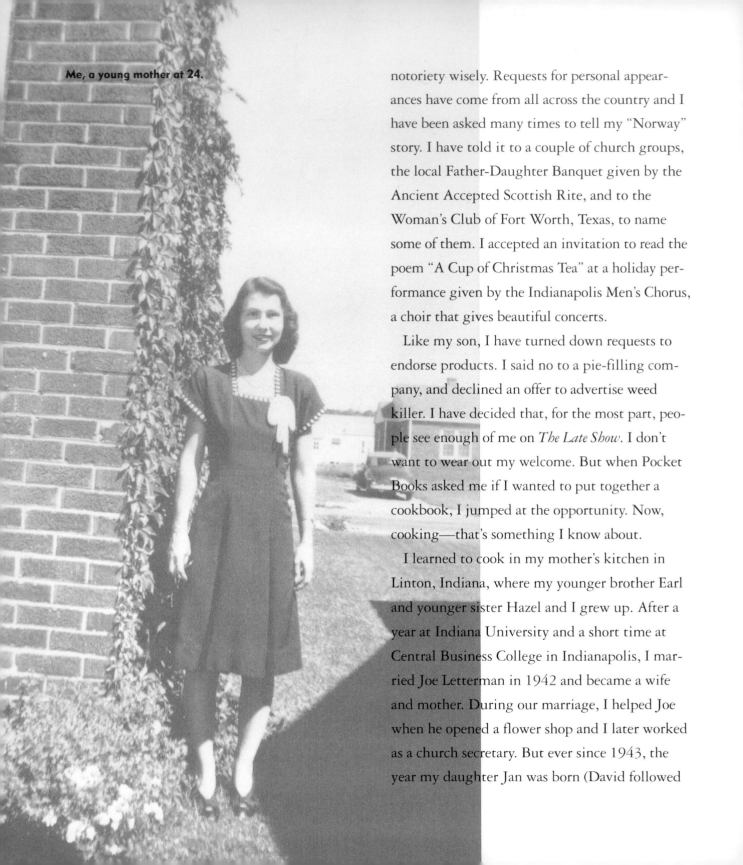

Me, a young mother at 24.

notoriety wisely. Requests for personal appearances have come from all across the country and I have been asked many times to tell my "Norway" story. I have told it to a couple of church groups, the local Father-Daughter Banquet given by the Ancient Accepted Scottish Rite, and to the Woman's Club of Fort Worth, Texas, to name some of them. I accepted an invitation to read the poem "A Cup of Christmas Tea" at a holiday performance given by the Indianapolis Men's Chorus, a choir that gives beautiful concerts.

Like my son, I have turned down requests to endorse products. I said no to a pie-filling company, and declined an offer to advertise weed killer. I have decided that, for the most part, people see enough of me on *The Late Show*. I don't want to wear out my welcome. But when Pocket Books asked me if I wanted to put together a cookbook, I jumped at the opportunity. Now, cooking—that's something I know about.

I learned to cook in my mother's kitchen in Linton, Indiana, where my younger brother Earl and younger sister Hazel and I grew up. After a year at Indiana University and a short time at Central Business College in Indianapolis, I married Joe Letterman in 1942 and became a wife and mother. During our marriage, I helped Joe when he opened a flower shop and I later worked as a church secretary. But ever since 1943, the year my daughter Jan was born (David followed in 1947, then Gretchen in 1955), I have been a full-time cook as well. I made sure that the entire family was together for at least one meal a day, and there were many special times spent in the kitchen with my children. I was never good at delegating—I'd rather do the work myself, I guess that's part of my impatience—but I loved having the kids underfoot.

When I baked cookies, I always set out a cookie sheet with unbaked cookie batter, and when the kids thought I wasn't looking, they would sneak up and eat the raw dough. When Jan was little, I would give her some flour, sugar, and water that she could mix up in a pan and pretend to make her own cookies, which she aptly named "Slum Goo." She just had a ball doing this. When David was a Boy Scout, he and I tested his campfire cooking equipment on the kitchen stove together. Nowadays I enjoy cooking with my grandchildren (Jan has a

BELOW: **Jan, 7, and David, 4, playing in the front yard. He's looking at her like she's good enough to eat.** RIGHT: **Jan and David with their dad in Fort Lauderdale, 1952**

grown son and daughter, Bill and Bryn; Gretchen has two young ones, Liam and Annagrace). Not long ago, when I was baking an apple pie, I let little Annagrace roll out the scraps of pie dough and sprinkle them with sugar and cinnamon. Then we baked them and she was so thrilled with her "cookies." It was thrilling for me, too. That's just what my own mother used to let me do on pie-baking days.

I think it's very important that parents teach their children how to cook at a very early age. It fosters independence and good feelings about themselves, and besides, they have fun doing it. Little boys especially should learn to cook so they can be self-sufficient as they mature.

Late last summer my grandson, Bill, called from New York. "Grandma," he said, "I have some beautiful peaches that are just begging to be put in a pie." Bill loves to cook, but he had never baked a pie, so I talked him through the whole process, crust and all. In a phone call two days later, Bill told me the pie was just wonderful. It's nice to know that my love of cooking is being handed down through the generations.

I recently read a story in *Newsweek* announcing that "home cooking is back." It said that sales of Crock-Pots (slow cookers) and pressure cookers were on the rise, and that "predictable, nonthreatening food" was back in style. I don't really know why this is. I like to think that the home-cooking movement reflects a movement back to basics, back to family. I hope it means that people are once again realizing the importance of family, regardless of that family's shape or size or variety.

I remember an evening at the end of my two weeks in Lillehammer; we were broadcasting on the Storgata (the street of stores), where a bunch of students and young people had gathered. It was so packed, we could barely move, and all the American kids were shouting, "Dave's mom, we love you!" I believe what they were really saying was that they love *their* moms. I represented Mom and family and home to them. The positive response to my appearances on David's show has nothing to do with my amateur abilities as a broadcaster. People enjoy seeing a mother and son together. It's that simple.

If basic, inexpensive home cooking is "trendy," as the magazines and cookbook experts say, then I've been trendy since July 18, 1921, the day I was born. I swear by my pressure cooker—always have. Years later, the Crock-Pot found a permanent place in my kitchen. And I have always shopped frugally. Being a "Depression kid," I learned to buy things on sale. But I never sacrificed quality for price—that's just not smart shopping. Raising my own family, I did a lot of

Dig the hats and wrinkled stockings! From left to right: Me, age 10, brother Earl, 9, and sister Hazel, 8, at home in Linton, Indiana. That's poor old Jack's head being held up by Earl.

OPPOSITE: **In Florida with grand-children Annagrace and Liam, in the summer of 1994.** RIGHT: **My hero, Hans, a member of the 82nd Airborne, in 1944.**

home canning, too. One year I canned 100 quarts of tomato juice from tomatoes grown in our own garden, as well as jars of green beans, peaches, and pickles.

Over the years, I've developed my own recipes. Like any home cook, I have added twists to Betty Crocker and adjusted recipes from the newspaper's food section to suit my own family's tastes. I have learned from my friends and I have gathered recipes on my travels. This book is as much a collection of other people's recipes as my own. Many of them come from my coworkers at Second Presbyterian Church. I was working there when Joe died unexpectedly of a heart attack in 1973, after David and Jan had left home and Gretchen was in high school. I couldn't have been in a better place with more caring friends. As I began going through my recipe files, I was amazed at how many recipes came from those gals. They're very special to me.

I asked David's staff, who have been so wonderful and supportive to me, for their favorite recipes. Some of the recipes I'm not sure will become regulars at my house, especially "Dog Jacks," but I'm grateful to have them here. I have also gathered many other recipes from little inns and bed-and-breakfasts that I have visited over the years. As I went through them and wrote letters to the proprietors asking permission to print them, I recalled many weekend getaways that I have made with my second husband, Hans, whom I married in 1983. Hans, who retired two years ago from his job as a structural engineer with an architectural firm, is a quiet, wonderful man—a perfect traveling companion in the car as well as in life. We enjoy the same foods and doing the same things, such as traveling, gardening, attending church activities, and visiting friends and family. He has a Purple Heart, from when his glider was shot down over Normandy on D-Day, and a real heart to match.

I hope that people using this cookbook will see themselves and their families in my stories. And I hope that it's useful. As I so often said to my kids when I set down their favorite birthday dinner or dessert: "Enjoy."

—*Dorothy, Carmel, Indiana, 1996*

An Old Poem from an Old Cookbook

BY OWEN MEREDITH (1831–91)

We may live without poetry, music and art.
We may live without conscience, and live
    without heart;
We may live without friends, we may live
    without books,
But civilized man cannot live without
    cooks.

He may live without books—what is
    knowledge but grieving?
He may live without hope—what is hope
    but deceiving?
He may live without love—what is
    passion but pining?
But where is the man who can live without
    dining?

As taken from the 1953 Second Presbyterian Church Cookbook.

FUN FOODS
SNACKS, DRINKS, AND COOKIES

I hear mothers say all the time that they don't let their kids snack between meals or that they teach kids not to snack, but I just don't think that's possible. Snacks are a necessity in a house with growing children. I think the best you can do is try to keep the snacks reasonably healthy and to not let the kids overdo it.

When David was in junior high, he had a paper route. Every day he'd set off on his bike at around four in the morning, and he'd be so hungry when he came home that he'd wolf down a snack of two or three peanut butter sandwiches, go back to bed, only to get up and have a breakfast of cereal, fruit juice, and toast a couple of hours later.

When Jan, David, and Gretchen came home from school, they would love to have french fries and milk. Sometimes the fries were homemade, but more often I'd just buy a box of frozen fries and stick them in the oven. Oatmeal raisin cookies and milk were also good after-school

snacks. I've always figured oatmeal cookies are fairly healthy, as far as sweets go. If you bake sixty cookies, the sugar and shortening is pretty thinly distributed, and with one or two eggs in the recipe spread out through the entire batch, you're not getting that much cholesterol. I read a recipe the other day that suggested using egg substitutes, and I thought, my goodness. I'm sure it doesn't taste as good.

During the '50s and '60s, because all the kids in the neighborhood seemed to congregate in our front yard, I made gallons and gallons of Kool-Aid. I carried it outside in a soup kettle because I didn't have a pitcher big enough and I ladled it out for them from the front porch. I guess they gravitated toward the Letterman house because Mom had snacks, or maybe it was just because I tolerated the children. Some mothers didn't want kids in their front yards. I thought it was kind of neat to have all the kids there, listening to their whoops and laughter while I worked in the house.

Selling Kool-Aid under the neighbors' buckeye tree. LEFT TO RIGHT: David, 6, Dick Brown, Jan, 9, and Sue Hollingsworth.

OVEN CARAMEL POPCORN

This is absolutely delicious. I often made it for my kids, and for the gals I used to work with during my sixteen years as secretary at Second Presbyterian Church. It never lasted long. If I recall correctly, the recipe came from the back of a calendar that our old insurance man left with me on one of his yearly visits.

2 cups packed brown sugar
2 sticks unsalted butter
½ cup white corn syrup
1 teaspoon salt
1 teaspoon baking soda
24 cups popped corn
Nonstick cooking spray

In a large heavy pot, over medium heat, boil sugar, butter, syrup, and salt for 5 minutes, stirring frequently. Remove from heat; stir in baking soda. Pour over popped corn, mixing well. Coat cookie sheet with nonstick spray. Spread popcorn evenly on cookie sheet. Place in 200-degree oven for 1 hour, stirring every 15 minutes. Remove from oven; cool. Store in covered container to keep crisp.

MAKES 24 SERVINGS.

CHEESE STRAWS

My good friend Anna Gail Dortch introduced me to these and I persuaded her to share this recipe. They freeze well, so you can always have them on hand for company.

2 cups minus 2 tablespoons flour
1 stick margarine
1 pound sharp cheddar cheese, grated
¼ teaspoon Tabasco sauce
Dash of salt

In a large bowl, combine all ingredients. Knead with hands (or put in food processor) until well blended. Pack mixture in cookie press and using a star-shaped tip, push through press in strips (straws) approximately 4–5 inches long on ungreased cookie sheet. Bake at 350 degrees for about 15 minutes. Remove from oven; cool. Return to oven at 200 degrees for ½ hour. Store in covered container; can be frozen.

MAKES ABOUT 3 DOZEN STRAWS.

FRIENDSHIP TEA

OPPOSITE: **Key lime spritzers: A cool drink with warm memories.**

This makes a tasty hot tea with a slice of lemon, but is equally nice in summer—over ice with a sprig of mint and slice of lemon, lime, or orange.

2 cups Tang instant breakfast drink
2 cups granulated sugar
1⅓ cups instant tea mix
1 teaspoon ground cinnamon
½ teaspoon ground cloves
2 3-ounce packages Wyler's Lemonade mix (optional)

Combine ingredients and pour through funnel into large glass container. Cover tightly. The dry mixture keeps for months in the refrigerator.

TO MAKE A QUART: use approximately ¼ cup of mix to 1 quart of water.

KEY LIME SPRITZER

A great summer drink. I found it in the food section of the *Indianapolis Star* more than 20 years ago. When Joe died in 1973, Gretchen was still in high school and we became even closer during that time. She and I took a vacation to Florida a couple of years after her dad's death. We sat on the beach at St. Petersburg, watching the sunset and enjoying key lime spritzers. We shared many good times there after that, and now that she and her family live in St. Petersburg, we still spend time together on the beach, playing with the children and taking long walks by the gulf.

½ cup dry white wine (Chardonnay or Chablis)
1 lime, halved (key lime or otherwise)
½ cup lemon-lime soda

Pour wine into tall glass filled with ice cubes. Add juice of half a lime and soda; stir. Slice the other lime half and use a slice to garnish glass.

MAKES 1 SERVING.

TEA PUNCH

This is a refreshing drink to serve on a warm, sunny day. For the life of me I can't remember who gave me this recipe.

> *4 family-size or 12 regular-size tea bags*
> *1 quart boiling water*
> *1¼ cups granulated sugar*
> *2 cups orange juice*
> *½ cup lemonade concentrate, undiluted*
> *4 cups water*

Steep tea bags in boiling water for 8 minutes. Remove tea bags. Add all other ingredients. Stir well. Serve hot or cold.

MAKES 12 SERVINGS.

ALMA'S OLD-FASHIONED SUGAR COOKIES

Alma Worthington, who was the food services director at Second Presbyterian for nearly 15 years, used to make these for us gals in the office in her spare time. She gave me the recipe years ago. I've passed it along to friends and it has become a favorite of theirs, too.

> *1 cup unsalted butter*
> *1 cup vegetable oil*
> *1 cup granulated sugar*
> *1 cup confectioners' sugar*
> *2 eggs*
> *1 teaspoon vanilla extract*
> *1 teaspoon baking soda*
> *4 cups flour*
> *1 teaspoon cream of tartar*
> *1 teaspoon salt*

Preheat oven to 375 degrees. In a large bowl, cream butter, oil, and sugars. Add eggs and vanilla. In another large bowl, sift dry ingredients, then add to wet ingredients and blend. Shape dough into small balls and place on ungreased cookie sheet. Flatten with a wet glass bottom dipped in sugar. Bake 12 minutes.

MAKES 8 DOZEN SMALL COOKIES.

Grilling burgers on our Coleman stove during a 1952 family vacation. LEFT TO RIGHT: Jan, 8, me, and David, 5.

The Generation Gap

On one of my broadcasts from Lillehammer, I was given the opportunity to read "The Late Show" Top Ten list. The topic for that evening was "Norwegians' Top 10 Nicknames for Americans." Gold medalist Dan Jansen was on hand to read the number-one nickname, "Bobbitteers." The rest, which I read, included "Knee-clubbers," "Opraholics," and "Gap-Tooth TV Boy."

"Actually, that's just you, David," I said after I read that last one. The line got a big laugh from the audience, because people seem to focus on the separation between David's top front teeth. He's always had it and it never occurred to us to fix it. No dentist ever said we should. His teeth are very straight. People have noted a similar gap in my teeth, but it wasn't always there. My teeth have separated only in the last few years, and I don't plan to start wearing braces to correct it.

Not so long ago, diet expert Richard Simmons was joking around on "The Late Show," and making a face like Alvin the Chipmunk. David accused Richard of making fun of him. "My folks couldn't afford to have my teeth fixed," David said. I was watching the show after it aired (I always tape "The Late Show" and watch it right after dinner the next evening), and I thought, "Oh, David!" Now it's my chance to tell the entire world: David went to the dentist regularly! But no, we decided not to fix the gap. I saw no reason to because it's part of David—one of the many things that make him so very special.

PEANUT BUTTER BLOSSOMS

OPPOSITE: **Just like his jack o' lanterns, David, 6, is missing a tooth or two!**

The kids loved these cookies when they were little, so when I sent David a batch of Christmas cookies one year after he had moved to New York, I included some. They're really just peanut butter cookies with a little something special (the Hershey's Kisses).

1¾ cups flour
1 teaspoon baking soda
½ teaspoon salt
½ cup shortening
½ cup peanut butter
½ cup granulated sugar
½ cup packed brown sugar
1 egg, unbeaten
1 teaspoon vanilla extract
1 package Hershey's Kisses

In a small bowl, sift flour, baking soda, and salt. Set aside. In a large bowl, cream together shortening, peanut butter, sugars, egg, and vanilla extract. Add dry mixture and blend thoroughly. Shape into balls, using 1 teaspoon dough. Roll balls in granulated sugar to coat and place on ungreased cookie sheet. Bake 10 minutes at 375 degrees. Remove from oven and press a Hershey's Kiss into each cookie. Return to oven and bake 2–5 minutes longer.

MAKES ABOUT 4 DOZEN.

READY... GET SET... APPETIZERS

Appetizers are for special occasions. I usually reserve these recipes for those times when company comes for dinner, and I always put some out at Thanksgiving and Christmas when the family is here. I like to serve appetizers on the kitchen table for my guests. That's less formal than arranging them on trays in the living room, and besides, inviting people into your kitchen makes them feel right at home. I believe appetizers were really invented so that the host doesn't have to have dinner ready the minute people walk in the door.

David, my 9-year-old all-star. The youngest kid on his Little League team, he batted .300 that year.

JAN'S SAUERKRAUT BALLS

This is my daughter Jan's crowning kitchen achievement. Maybe I should call them "Jan's Famous Sauerkraut Balls," since you may have read about them in *Entertainment Weekly* magazine. While a reporter was interviewing David at his office, David's former agent, Mike Ovitz, arrived. According to the story in the magazine, Mr. Ovitz had been served Jan's sauerkraut balls on an earlier visit and hadn't cared for them. So on this occasion the *Late Show* staff put out caviar for him instead. All I can say is, Mr. Ovitz has wonderful taste in his clients, but not in appetizers. Jan has served these to me many times, and they are so good.

½ pound ground ham
½ pound ground pork
½ pound corned beef
4 tablespoons chopped onion
2 tablespoons fresh chopped parsley
¼ cup shortening
2 cups flour
2 cups milk
1 teaspoon dry mustard
1 teaspoon salt
2 pounds sauerkraut, drained
Flour
2 eggs, slightly beaten
Fine dry bread crumbs

Add meats, onion, and parsley to food processor. Process until well mixed. In a large skillet, melt half of the shortening and sauté mixture, stirring constantly until browned. Blend in flour; slowly stir in milk and seasonings. Cook until mixture is light and fluffy (mixture will be stiff at first; it becomes fluffy as it cooks). Allow to cool. Add sauerkraut and stir; put mixture in food processor again and blend. Return mixture to skillet and cook, stirring constantly, until quite thick. Cool. Roll into walnut-size balls. Dip in flour, then in beaten eggs, and coat in bread crumbs. (May be frozen at this point.) In a large skillet, melt the other half of the shortening and fry until golden. Serve with a honey mustard.

MAKES ABOUT 100 SAUERKRAUT BALLS.

TEX-MEX DIP

This is my old standby when I need something for church pitch-in dinners. It's simple to make, but looks so pretty with the variegated colors all layered on a big platter.

3 medium-size ripe avocados, peeled and pitted
2 tablespoons fresh lemon juice
½ teaspoon salt
¼ teaspoon black pepper
1 cup sour cream (or substitute light variety)
½ cup mayonnaise (or substitute light variety)
1 package taco seasoning mix
2 cans plain or flavored jalapeño bean dip
1 large bunch green onions, with stems, chopped
2 or 3 medium tomatoes, peeled, seeded, and coarsely chopped
1 7-ounce can pitted black olives, sliced
8 ounces sharp cheddar cheese, shredded

   In a small bowl, mash avocados with lemon juice, salt, and pepper. In another small bowl, combine sour cream, mayonnaise, and taco seasoning. On a large oval serving platter, spread bean dip to cover platter. On top of that, spread a layer of avocado mixture. Add a layer of the mayonnaise/sour cream/taco seasoning mix. Sprinkle onions, tomatoes, and olives on the top. Cover with cheese. Serve either chilled or at room temperature.

MAKES ABOUT 6 CUPS.

OPPOSITE: **Second Presbyterian Church in Indianapolis.**

CRABMEAT CANAPÉS

My friend Pat Foster shared this recipe with me in 1991 when we were cochairpersons of the annual Women's Bazaar at the Second Presbyterian Church. This event raises money for the church's benevolent fund by selling all kinds of home-cooked food, antiques, kitchen wares, and anything that's in fairly good shape. Together, we raised $38,000 and became good friends in the process. When Hans and I visit Pat and her husband, Dick, at their place in Wisconsin, she sometimes has these canapés waiting for us when we arrive.

8 slices white bread, crusts removed
¼ cup unsalted butter
1 can flaked crabmeat
1 teaspoon onion juice
2 tablespoons bottled hot horseradish
½ teaspoon salt
¼ cup mayonnaise
1 tablespoon fresh lemon juice
Parmesan cheese

Using cookie cutter or juice glass, cut bread into rounds or cut into squares. In a large skillet, melt butter. Brown bread pieces on one side. Mix remaining ingredients except cheese. Pile on toasted side of bread. Sprinkle with cheese. Arrange canapés on greased cookie sheet and broil until delicately brown, about 2 minutes. Serve hot.

MAKES 32 CANAPÉS.

Tom Townsend's Cheese Spread

Tom, a friend and member of Second Presbyterian, used to make this spread for Christmas gifts. Everyone loved it so much that the church now sells it at the annual bazaar. Every year, men from the church, including Hans, volunteer two afternoons to help make it in huge commercial mixers. And Hans always makes sure a jar or two ends up in our refrigerator.

1 pound sharp, cold-pack, spreadable
   cheddar cheese*
$^1/_2$ cup mayonnaise*
$^1/_4$ cup very hot horseradish*
$^1/_4$ teaspoon hot, dry mustard
7 drops Tabasco sauce
3 drops Worcestershire sauce

Mix well, then whip with whisk.

MAKES 2 CUPS.

*Cheese can be Land O Lakes, Wispride, Merrywood, or Kaukana Club.
*Use a good grade of mayonnaise, such as Hellmann's Real.
*For a fresh and hot horseradish, I suggest Thor's Extra Hot.

David, 5, with a friend. He's a cute little guy, isn't he? (David, I mean.)

HEART-WARMING SOUPS

Any mother will tell you that raising kids without soup is just about a mission impossible. When Jan, David, or Gretchen had been sick and were getting back on solid food, I always started them off on plain beef broth with a slice of bread. When they were back at school they always came home for lunch, because their school was just down the street from our house. In case I didn't have a homemade soup prepared, I kept cans of good old reliable Campbell's and Lipton mixes on hand. I used to put canned bean-and-bacon soup through the blender to make it nice and smooth. Of course, the following recipes are a bit more trouble than opening a can of Campbell's, but I promise they're worth it.

CREAM OF MUSHROOM

I concocted this soup over the years. I call this kind of recipe "by guess and by golly"—looking at various cookbooks and adapting the soup to my own taste.

4 tablespoons unsalted butter
1 pound fresh mushrooms, sliced
6 scallions sliced, or 1 large onion, chopped
¼ cup flour
1 teaspoon salt
¼ teaspoon white pepper
1¼ cups water
1 can unsalted chicken broth
1 cup half-and-half, or milk (even skim will do)
Fresh chopped parsley

In a medium saucepan, melt butter. Add mushrooms and scallions or onion and sauté until tender. Stir in flour, salt, and pepper. Cook over low heat until smooth. Stir in water and broth. Heat to boiling. Add half-and-half and heat just to boiling (do not boil). Garnish with fresh parsley.

MAKES 4 SERVINGS.

GAZPACHO

About 10 years ago, I found the Waterford Inne, in Waterford, Maine, listed in a book about romantic inns. That's why Hans and I decided to go there. It's a lovely place, a restored nineteenth-century farmhouse located on twenty-five acres near the New Hampshire border, and we've now visited it three times. They raise many of their own fresh vegetables right on the site, and use them to make this gazpacho.

1 large cucumber, peeled, seeded, and coarsely chopped
¼–½ cup bread crumbs
2 tablespoons extra-virgin olive oil
1 medium onion, chopped
2 large garlic cloves
¼ cup dry parsley flakes
3 large tomatoes, peeled, seeded, and coarsely chopped
1 green bell pepper, seeded and coarsely chopped
2 24-ounce cans V8 vegetable juice
Garnish with diced green bell pepper, cucumber chunks, and fresh basil leaves

In food processor with steel blade, combine cucumber, bread crumbs, and oil. Process until smooth. Add onion, garlic cloves, parsley flakes, tomatoes, and green pepper and process. Add V8 vegetable juice and blend. Garnish with diced green bell pepper, cucumber chunks, and basil. Serve chilled or at room temperature.

MAKES 12 SERVINGS.

LENTIL SOUP

This recipe comes from daughter Jan. The beef bouillon and vinegar make it different and delicious. Pair it with some crusty bread and a salad for a wonderful meal on a cold night.

1 cup lentils, picked over and washed
5 cups cold water
4 slices bacon, diced
½ cup chopped onion
¼ cup chopped carrot
1 medium tomato, peeled, seeded, and chopped
3 tablespoons unsalted butter
3 tablespoons flour
2 teaspoons salt
2 tablespoons red wine vinegar
1 can beef bouillon, undiluted

In a large saucepan, over medium heat, simmer lentils and water for 1 hour. In a medium skillet, over medium heat, fry the bacon until crisp. Add onion, carrot, and tomato and sauté for 5 minutes. When lentils are done, add bacon and vegetables. In a medium skillet, over medium heat, melt butter. Stir in flour, salt, vinegar, and bouillon. Bring to a boil and add to lentils. Cover and cook 30 minutes.

MAKES 4 SERVINGS.

Variation: Add ½ pound smoked sausage, or kielbasa, cut in slices, and cook 10 more minutes.

Tomato Celery Soup

This is one of my favorite dishes from the Shaker Village of Pleasant Hill near Harrodsburg, Kentucky, which Hans and I visit at least twice a year. The village sits on 27,000 perfectly kept acres with fields of wildflowers, and has a complex of buildings that houses guests. The Village was established by a group of Shakers in 1805, closed in 1910, then renovated in 1961. Today it's the largest restored village of its kind in the country. Every spring we like to take one of the wildflower walks that the village offers, and, of course, enjoy the tomato celery soup in the dining hall. The recipe for this soup (as well as the Pumpkin Muffins on page 127) can also be found in the Shaker Village cookbook, *We Make You Kindly Welcome*, by Elizabeth Kremer.

2 tablespoons unsalted butter
1 small onion, chopped
½ cup finely chopped celery
1 10½-ounce can tomato soup
1 soup can of water
1 teaspoon minced parsley
1 tablespoon fresh lemon juice
1 teaspoon granulated sugar
¼ teaspoon salt
1 teaspoon black pepper
Whipped cream, unsweetened
Chopped parsley

In medium saucepan, over medium heat, melt butter. Sauté onion and celery until translucent. Add tomato soup, water, parsley, lemon juice, sugar, salt, and pepper. Simmer 5 minutes. Celery will remain crisp. Top with dollop of unsweetened whipped cream and chopped parsley.

MAKES 2 SERVINGS.

HOUSE SPECIAL CHICKEN NOODLE SOUP WITH HOMEMADE NOODLES

This soup is my own recipe, but I learned to make the noodles from my mother. Homemade noodles are so much better than store-bought because they taste lighter and are more tender. It has taken me a lot of practice over the years to be able to get them right. I've tried to teach daughter Jan and her daughter, Bryn, how to make the noodles. They still say that they can't do it. That's OK. I'm always happy to make noodles for them. The noodles are good for more than chicken noodle soup. I serve them with beef stroganoff, and with turkey gravy on Thanksgiving. I don't think you've really had noodles until you've had them homemade.

STOCK

4 pounds chicken backs, necks, and wings, or a 3- to 4-pound whole frying chicken, cut up
4 quarts cold water
3 ribs celery with leaves, chopped
1 large onion, chopped

OVERLEAF: **Homemade noodles. Practice makes perfect.**

In a large stockpot, add chicken and water. Bring to a boil on medium-low heat, then cook for 15 minutes; skim. Add vegetables, cover, and simmer for 2 hours. Discard chicken parts. (If using whole chicken parts, remove and refrigerate to use in another dish.) Strain stock and chill for 6 hours, or up to 2 days. Skim fat and simmer for 30 minutes. Can be cooled and frozen if not used immediately.

MAKES ABOUT 8 CUPS OF STOCK.

NOODLES

2 eggs
½ teaspoon salt
1 cup all-purpose or bread flour (bread flour is best)
¼ cup water

In a small bowl, beat eggs with salt. In a large bowl, pour flour and make a well in center. Mix in eggs gradually. Add water 1 teaspoon at a time. Knead until smooth and elastic, adding more flour or water if necessary. Divide dough into thirds. Roll out one part at a time on pastry cloth into a thin rectangle and let dry a bit. Fold dough lengthwise into thirds and cut into noodles with a sharp knife. Separate noodles and place on tea towels. Let dry completely. Freeze in airtight container or plastic bags if not to be used immediately.

MAKES 4 SERVINGS.*

While noodles are drying, cook 2–3 chicken breasts until tender; remove meat from bones. Add noodles and chicken to boiling stock. Cook for 20–25 minutes or until tender.

*If you wish to double the noodle recipe, do not simply double the ingredients. For a larger batch of noodles, use 3 egg yolks and 1 whole egg plus 1 teaspoon salt, 2 cups flour, and ½ cup water. Makes 8 servings.

Note: Noodles can be broken into smaller pieces, if desired.

VEGETABLE SOUP

One of my own specialties. I learned how to make vegetable soup from my mother, but it's very difficult to write down a recipe for vegetable soup because it's different every time I make it. Of course, that's the beauty of it. Have fun with it. Put in whatever vegetables you like; it's always tasty and nourishing.

STOCK
4–5 pounds beef short ribs
1 onion, chopped
2 ribs celery with leaves, chopped
2 carrots, chopped
1 sprig parsley
2 bouillon cubes, dissolved in 2 cups hot water

Roast ribs on baking pan in 450-degree oven until brown, approximately 30 minutes, turning to brown all sides. Then transfer ribs to stockpot, and add onion, celery, carrots, and parsley. Add enough boiling water to cover ribs. Pour fat off baking pan and deglaze pan with hot water. Pour over ribs in stockpot. Add dissolved bouillon cubes, cover, and simmer for 2–3 hours until ribs are tender (the meat will fall off the bones). Remove ribs and vegetables from stock. Set ribs aside to cool. Discard vegetables. Refrigerate stock (overnight is fine). Remove meat from bones and refrigerate. The next day remove congealed fat from stock and return meat to stock. I usually save part of the meat for beef barbecue. Add whatever vegetables you have—broccoli, cauliflower, turnips, lima beans, cabbage, tomatoes, etc. Salt to taste. Let simmer until vegetables are tender.

MAKES ABOUT 8 CUPS OF STOCK.

Note: This is even better the next day. If you are going to freeze some of this soup, don't use potatoes. They can be added when you defrost the soup to use later.

UNFORGETTABLE FRENCH ONION SOUP

From Debra Beasley. She and her husband, John, own the beautiful Beasley Orchard in Danville, Indiana, where Hans and I get a lot of our fresh sweet corn in the summer. Beasley's also offers tours showing how apples and pumpkins are grown. During the apple tour, you get to pick your own apples in the orchard and see how they are pressed for cider. The pumpkins are plump and ripe, ready to be transformed into smiling jack-o'-lanterns for Halloween, or into velvety pies for Thanksgiving. Mrs. Beasley puts out a newsletter, *The Cider Press*, which is where I discovered this onion soup. It really is unforgettable.

6 cups beef broth
2 large onions, thinly sliced
1 cup sliced mushrooms
½ cup sliced almonds
3 tablespoons unsalted butter
2 tablespoons dry sherry (optional)
2 teaspoons Worcestershire sauce
2 cups homemade or store-bought croutons
1½ cups shredded Swiss cheese, or 6 ounces sliced

In a large saucepan, over medium heat, combine beef broth, onions, mushrooms, almonds, butter, sherry (if you like) and Worcestershire sauce. Bring to a boil. Reduce heat. Cover and simmer for 10 minutes or until the onions are tender. Ladle the soup into 4 microwave-safe or broiler-safe bowls. Top with croutons and cheese. Cook in microwave or under the broiler until the cheese melts. (Allow about 2½ minutes on high power in the microwave.)

MAKES 4 MAIN DISH SERVINGS.

Note: Don't leave out the mushrooms and almonds—they make all the difference.

SALAD WAYS

I remember Mother's coleslaw and her lettuce salads. We always had cabbage and lettuce fresh from the garden. We grew Black Seeded Simpson in the summertime, and settled for iceberg during the winter. Since Dad couldn't stand mayonnaise, Mother made a hot bacon dressing for both coleslaw and lettuce salads.

I make my own salad dressing, too—using red wine or balsamic vinegar and some good extra-virgin olive oil, a bit of salt, and some freshly ground pepper. It's nothing fancy, but I've never had any complaints, and I never had a problem getting my kids to eat their salad. In my home, the salad has almost always been served with the rest of the meal. It's nice to be able to serve the salad first, but when you're cooking for a family and trying to coordinate everything in a hurry, it usually doesn't work out that way. I especially enjoy the wide variety of lettuces that are available—romaine, endive, Boston red, red leaf. These days the list is endless.

Investigating
mushrooms at
Atlas Supermarket
in Broad Ripple.

LEEKS
1.49

ARTICHOKES
1.69

ROMA
TOMATOES
89¢

YELLOW
SQUASH
$1.29
LB

ZUCCHINI
SQUASH
89¢
LB

YELLOW
CORN
3 FOR $1.79

WHITE
CORN
3 FOR $1.79

Campbells
Fresh
Mushrooms

German-Style Potato Salad

Another dish prepared by guess and by golly. I cook the potatoes in the pressure cooker, but I tend to vary the amounts of sugar and vinegar when I make it. It just depends on your taste.

4 medium potatoes, peeled and quartered
4 slices bacon, diced
¼ cup packed brown sugar or granulated sugar
2 tablespoons flour
½ cup water
¼ cup vinegar
1 teaspoon salt
⅛ teaspoon black pepper
1 small onion, sliced

Pressure cooker: Cook potatoes in 1 cup of water for about 10 minutes after the pressure is up. Drain, cool, and dice.

Conventional method: In a medium saucepan cover potatoes with water, and cook over medium heat for about 20–25 minutes, or until tender. Cool, drain, and dice. In a medium skillet, over medium heat, fry bacon until crisp. Drain on paper towel. Reserve two tablespoons of bacon drippings, and then add sugar, flour, water, vinegar, salt, pepper, and onion. Cook, stirring frequently until mixture thickens, approximately 5 minutes. Add bacon. Pour bacon and sauce mixture onto diced potatoes and stir. Serve warm.

MAKES 4 SERVINGS.

House Special Hot Chicken Salad

Another recipe from Alma Worthington. Long before I started compiling my cookbook, my editor from Pocket Books, Sue Carswell, flew out to Indiana to talk to me about the book project. I decided to impress her with this recipe. It was autumn and we were sitting in my enclosed porch as the leaves were falling to the ground. I was nervous about her reaction, hoping to prove that I was a good cook. Out of the corner of my eye, I saw her merely picking at the water chestnuts and celery. As I cleared the table and walked back into my kitchen, I wondered to myself how I could ask her what was wrong with my cooking. There I was, about to embark on a cookbook and my editor obviously didn't care for my food. I was afraid that the whole project was going to be canceled! Finally I diplomatically asked her if there was anything that should be changed in the recipe. Only then did she reveal that she was a vegetarian. I quickly changed our evening dinner reservations to an Italian restaurant. I had planned to take her out for prime rib!

BELOW: **Hot chicken salad. My editor won't be having this dish anytime soon!**

1 cup cooked rice
1 cup cooked diced chicken
1 cup chopped celery
1 can cream of chicken soup, undiluted
¾ cup mayonnaise (I use light, but not fat-free)
¾ cup sliced almonds or water chestnuts
2 tablespoons chopped onion
Crushed cornflake crumbs
Butter

In an 8-inch-square baking dish, combine all ingredients, except cornflake crumbs. Top with crushed cornflakes, dot with butter. Bake at 350 degrees for 45 minutes.

MAKES 4 SERVINGS.

LILLY SALAD

From my longtime friend Virginia Link. I've known Virginia all my life and we often exchange recipes. This one has been in her family for generations, and Virginia's mother, Katie, always made it for Easter dinner. When Katie entertained her women's club, she served it over angel food cake.

SALAD
1 pound miniature marshmallows
4 large oranges, peeled and cut into pieces
1 large can pineapple chunks, drained

DRESSING
4 egg yolks
1 cup milk
1 cup pineapple juice
2 tablespoons granulated sugar
2 tablespoons flour

WHIPPED CREAM
1 pint heavy cream
2 tablespoons granulated sugar

In a large mixing bowl, mix the marshmallows and fruit. Set aside. Combine dressing ingredients in a medium saucepan, and cook over medium heat. Cool. Add to fruit. In separate bowl, beat cream and sugar to whipped consistency and fold into salad mixture. Place in your prettiest serving bowl and let stand overnight in refrigerator. This salad will keep for several days.

MAKES 8–10 SERVINGS.

MANDARIN ORANGE AND ALMOND SALAD

From Barb Lucas, a home economist who used to volunteer answering phones at Second Presbyterian.

1 head iceberg lettuce, torn into small pieces
½ head romaine lettuce, torn into small pieces
6 green onions, sliced
2 cups chopped celery
½ cup slivered almonds
¼ cup granulated sugar
1 16-ounce can mandarin oranges, drained
1 pound fresh mushrooms, sliced (optional)

DRESSING
½ cup extra-virgin olive oil
¼ cup red wine vinegar
¼ cup granulated sugar
2 tablespoons fresh minced parsley
1 teaspoon salt
Freshly ground black pepper
Dash of Tabasco sauce

In a large serving bowl, add lettuces, onion, and celery. Toss. Refrigerate. In a small skillet, over low heat, stir almonds in sugar until lightly toasted. Cool. In a vinaigrette bottle, shake dressing ingredients and refrigerate at least 1 hour. Toss with salad greens. Add or top with almonds, mandarin oranges, and mushrooms, if desired.

MAKES 8 SERVINGS.

SHELL SALAD

From my friend Lyn Milan, a secretary at Second Presbyterian. It's a good dish to take on picnics or family reunions.

1 8-ounce package shell macaroni, large or small, cooked and drained
1½ cups thinly sliced zucchini
1½ cups peeled, seeded, and diced tomatoes
¼ cup chopped parsley, fresh or dried
1 teaspoon each oregano and basil
¼ teaspoon garlic powder
1 8-ounce bottle Italian dressing

In a large serving bowl, mix together and marinate at least 2 hours (overnight is better).

MAKES 4 SERVINGS.

SOUVENIR SALAD DRESSING

From the Hotel Rica, Lillehammer, Norway. It's no wonder I didn't collect more recipes while working in Lillehammer (see page 70). We barely had time to eat! But each evening, after we had put in a long day, and before we hooked up to the satellite for the live broadcast, I was able to put my feet up and have some soup and salad at the Hotel Rica, where we were staying. I asked the waiter if he would get the salad dressing recipe from the chef while I was there because it was so unusual and just jumping with flavors. I've adapted it a bit to include whatever fresh herbs are available. The hotel dining room splashed it on a large variety of salad greens—watercress, endive, and escarole, with cherry tomatoes, carrots, and cucumbers. I collected Olympic pins during my stay in Lillehammer, but this dressing is a wonderful souvenir as well. It brings back good memories.

⅓ cup balsamic vinegar
⅔ extra-virgin olive oil.
1 teaspoon each fresh, finely chopped taragon, chives, parsley, basil, chervil
Freshly ground black pepper

In a bottle, combine all ingredients. Shake well before serving.

MAKES 1 CUP.

Gretchen and her husband Bill and their little ones: Annagrace, 4 1/2, and Liam, almost 2.

GRETCHEN'S SALAD DRESSING

My daughter Gretchen is so great at throwing things together, even with her busy schedule as a features editor for *The St. Petersburg Times* and running a household. But she finds the time to fix this dressing for me whenever I visit.

2 tablespoons fresh lemon, lime, or grapefruit juice
2 tablespoons red wine vinegar
1/2 teaspoon Dijon mustard
4 tablespoons vegetable oil
4 tablespoons extra-virgin olive oil
4–5 drops Tabasco sauce
1 garlic clove, kept whole
Salt and pepper to taste

In a small bowl, mix vinegar and mustard. Whisk in remaining ingredients.

MAKES 3/4 CUP.

Dining by Headlight

When Joe and I took our kids on vacations, I always made sure that we had a cooler full of picnic-type foods and snacks with us. In the evenings, we'd eat out, but the rest of the time I thought the kids were better off eating what I had prepared for them. I would wrap up a bunch of ham sandwiches and put some potato salad in a wide-mouthed jar. Cereal was always on hand, and we'd stop and get milk, so the kids could have that for breakfast. Once, on the way to Montreal, the wind got so fierce during a roadside breakfast that all of David's cornflakes blew right out of his bowl!

Of course, I'd bake lots of cookies for the trips. I can remember getting barely as far as the south side of Indianapolis when David would declare he was so hungry that he couldn't wait until lunch. He knew those chocolate chip cookies were in the trunk, so we'd stop and dig out a couple for him.

Before Gretchen was born, when Jan and David were still little, Joe and I drove with them to Fort Lauderdale on vacation. For that trip, we took along a Coleman stove so we could grill hamburgers for supper. Down in Daytona Beach, the mosquitoes were unbearable! Joe

and I sprayed some mosquito repellent on ourselves and fixed breakfast just as quickly as we could while Jan and David waited in the car. The children rolled the window down just enough so that I could pass poached eggs and toast to them on paper plates.

All three kids were good travelers, but when Gretchen was a little girl, she was nervous about taking her first plane trip. She was going to Denver with just Joe and me, because we were going to attend a florist retailers convention there. Jan and David, who were both older and out of the house by this time, scared Gretchen silly by telling her that if anything happened to her, they were going to use the insurance money to buy a Dairy Queen. Poor little Gretchen just knew that plane was going to crash.

These days, when Hans and I want to get away, we very often travel by plane. But we also like to just get in the car and take off to spend the night at an inn or a bed-and-breakfast. For a light lunch while traveling by car, we like to stop at McDonald's for a salad and coffee. (Also, their rest rooms are always nice and clean.) As you will see by the number of recipes I've collected from various inns, food is always a top priority on our travels.

STRAWBERRY VINAIGRETTE

OPPOSITE: **Jan, 8, and David, 5, on a family vacation. Our chariot is a 1949 Chevy.**

This recipe is from Steve Coakley, executive chef at Henry's in the Strater, a wonderful old Victorian hotel that was completed in 1888 in Durango, Colorado. Hans and I visited the Strater in 1995 when we rode excursion trains through Wyoming, Utah, Colorado, and Idaho. Their salad dressing goes especially well with mixed baby greens and endive. Whenever I make it at home, it's as good as I remember it from our dinner at the hotel.

1 pint strawberries, stems removed
½ cup strawberry vinegar (available in gourmet food stores; it's pricey but worth it)
¼ cup honey*
¾ cup extra-virgin olive oil
¼ cup good vegetable oil
Pinch of white pepper

In a food processor or blender, combine strawberries and vinegar and puree until smooth. Add honey. With food processor running, add oils through feed tube and continue processing until completely emulsified. Add white pepper.

MAKES 2 ½ CUPS.

* You may need more honey, depending on the ripeness of the strawberries.

©MARY ANN CARTER

Dorothy of the North

I was visiting Gretchen in St. Petersburg when I got the phone call from "The Late Show" producer Maria Pope asking me to cover the 1994 Winter Olympics in Lillehammer, Norway. Whenever David wants me to do something on the show, one of the producers usually calls. He figures that if I really don't want to do it, I'll have an easier time saying no to someone besides him. Of course, I was so excited about the idea of going to the Olympics, and told Maria that Hans and I would love to go. Then the phone call from David came, telling me all the reasons why I shouldn't take the assignment.

"Mom, it'll be cold in Norway," he warned.

"We can handle that, David," I said.

"And you'll have to eat reindeer," he said.

"Well, that's okay," I told him. "We had reindeer chili in Alaska."

He wasn't really trying to talk me out of it. That was just David being protective. As it turned out, I could have used some protection. A few days before we were scheduled to leave, I took a nasty fall outside our travel agent's office. We had just made arrangements for a Caribbean trip, and wouldn't you know I ended up with eight stitches on my eyebrow. Early on the morning we were to leave for Indianapolis International Airport, the stitches were removed, but I was left with the worst black eye you ever saw. At Newark Airport a CBS makeup gal was waiting to cover the bruise that had spread all over one side of my face, because the network had asked us to get some video of me on the flight to Norway. (Hans took his home video camera and shot me sitting with the pilots, wearing an officer's hat, and deeply engrossed in learning about the instrument panel. It was aired later in the week on "The Late Show.") While we were working in Lillehammer, our driver, Jay Simpson, kept a compact in his pocket so I could touch up when it came time to roll the camera. Nobody ever realized that I was an absolute mess under all that makeup. But, by hook or by crook, I wasn't about to disappoint Dave's audience.

On my second full day there, I did my interview with Hillary Clinton, who put me right at ease. She was so nice. With the network's footage ready to go, David introduced me and I was piped in live by satellite. Before we aired the tape of Mrs. Clinton, David asked me how the food was, and whether they ate a lot of reindeer in Norway. I told him "not a lot."

Of course, I eventually did eat some reindeer and David wanted to know all about it. When he asked me about it on the air, I told him it tasted a little bit like filet mignon.

"What else do you eat with reindeer?" he asked.

"They served it with a mushroom sauce," I said.

"Well, you know, anything's not so bad with mushroom sauce," he said. "I learned that from you, Mom."

He certainly did. I liked the reindeer steak almost as much as I enjoyed my ride on a sled pulled by reindeer. The McSalmon burgers at McDonald's, however, were bad news. I had a bite or two of the burger for the camera, but Hans had to finish it.

Our days were long and exhausting and we got by on five or six hours sleep if we were lucky. But the adrenaline kept me from getting very tired, and the excitement just kept building over the course of our two weeks there. The broadcast in New York started taping at 5:30 P.M. — which was 11:30 P.M. Norway time — so it was usually midnight or so by the time I spoke to David via satellite. I would speak to him live for a minute or so, then they'd air segments and interviews that we had taped during the day. Steve O'Donnell, the writer, and Maria Pope helped me through the interviews. While I was talking to gold medalist Tommy Moe, Steve instructed me to ask, "What kind of name is Moe?" I didn't really want to ask that because I thought it was too personal a question, but I did everything they asked. And, of course, the line got a big laugh from the audience.

Steve and Maria came up with wonderful gags for each interview. Tommy got a canned ham from me.

I gave Bonnie Blair a fifteen-pound chunk of Jarlsberg cheese (we had to carry it around all day!). My only difficult interview was Nancy Kerrigan. She's very serious and I don't think she cares much for interviews. We were in her hotel, and Steve kept telling me to offer her some cocoa and she kept saying "No thanks." I tried to get Tonya Harding's attention backstage at the ice-skating rink, but she ignored me, so we simply aired tape of her looking away as I called, "Tonya! Tonya!" I really appreciate now what David does. I knew he worked hard, but I didn't know how hard until I did the same type of thing during my stay in Lillehammer.

MAIN DISHES

When Jan and David were very young, I would occasionally prepare fried chicken, but I preferred serving beef or pork at dinnertime, so those are the meat dishes my family enjoyed.

When I was growing up, Sundays were special. Very often Mother would fix a Swiss steak surrounded by carrots, potatoes, and onions. She'd put it in the oven before church and it was ready when we got home. Sometimes she'd get up a little earlier and put together a lemon meringue pie to go with it. But her oven-fried chicken was always one of my favorites. I think it was so tasty because it was so fresh. I love it so much that I've made it the House Special in this section...as a nod to Mother, and a thanks for the wonderful memories.

My dad with his chickens, back home in Linton, Indiana.
OPPOSITE: Hans working his magic with some bratwurst.

Less Salt Can Be More

Use sea salt coarse crystals (sel de mer gros) when seasoning foods. It takes less salt to get the flavor you need.

BEEF ROULADES

It's funny how certain foods can jog one's memory. At one point after Mother died in 1969, Dad wasn't feeling well, so he stayed with Joe and me for three weeks. When he was better, David and I took him back home to Linton and I made beef roulades in my mother's old kitchen, where she had taught me how to make them many years before. We had to stop at the grocery store to get the ingredients because with Mother gone, Dad's cupboard stayed pretty bare. I whipped up the roulades in 15 minutes and they were delicious. "Mom, where did you learn to cook like this?" David asked.

I said, "David, I learned to cook in this kitchen."

"They're good," Dad told him, "but your mom can't cook like your grandmother did."

1½ pounds boneless round steak
Salt and pepper
Flour to coat
Bacon slices
1 onion, cut into eighths
Dill pickle spears
Carrot sticks (optional)
¼ cup olive oil
1 can beef broth
1½ teaspoons flour
1½ teaspoons water

Pound steak until very thin; sprinkle with salt, pepper, and flour. Cut into pieces approximately 4 x 2 inches. Lay about ⅓ slice bacon on each piece of round steak. Add onion piece, dill pickle spear, and carrot. Roll up and fasten with toothpicks.

Pressure cooker: In uncovered cooker, brown roulades in hot olive oil. Add broth, cover, and after the pressure comes up, reduce heat a bit and cook for 15 minutes and let pressure return to normal. Remove meat. Mix flour with water and add to cooker to thicken gravy.

Conventional method: In a large skillet, over medium heat, heat oil. Add meat and brown. Add broth, cover, and let cook 30–35 minutes. Remove meat and mix flour and water in skillet until gravy thickens. Serve with noodles or mashed potatoes.

MAKES 6 SERVINGS.

Grandma Burgers

That's what my grandchildren call them. They taste wonderful because I don't skimp on the trimmings. I pile my burgers with lettuce and tomato until they almost look like the Dagwood sandwiches from the comic strip, nice and fat and juicy. The onions and bread crumbs add a lot to the recipe. So many times people just put a plain hamburger patty on the grill, but I think the meat needs a little dressing up.

1 pound lean ground
   beef
1 small onion, chopped
1 slice dry bread,
   crumbled (I use oat-
   meal bread)
1 egg, well beaten
1 teaspoon salt
4 hamburger buns

In a large bowl, mix ingredients well and form into 4 hamburgers. Cook on nonstick griddle or coat outdoor grill with cooking spray and grill.

MAKES 4 SERVINGS.

CHILI SAUCE

This was Mother's recipe, and I've used it for years. She also made homemade ketchup, but I preferred this. I love it on poached or scrambled eggs or with hamburgers. It's good in shrimp cocktail sauce, too, and it smells wonderful when it's cooking.

20 large tomatoes, peeled, seeded, and chopped
6–8 large onions, chopped
10 medium green bell peppers, chopped
3 tablespoons salt
2 cups granulated sugar
2 teaspoons ground ginger
1 teaspoon celery seed
½ teaspoon black pepper
1 teaspoon ground cinnamon
1 cup cider vinegar
1–2 hot peppers, seeded and chopped (optional)

In a food processor or blender, add all ingredients. Pulse to chopped consistency. (Don't process too long; mixture will get mushy.) In a large kettle, combine all ingredients and bring to a boil, then simmer for an hour or more until desired consistency. Pour in hot sterilized jars and seal.

MAKES 3 PINTS. (I use half-pint jars.)

CHOP SUEY

My Aunt Hazel, Dad's sister, who lived in Chicago, made this chop suey for my family back in 1933, when we visited her during the World's Fair. Called "A Century of Progress," the fair was really spectacular and I got to take my very first escalator ride. Plus, Aunt Hazel made this chop suey for us. My mother got the recipe and made it over the years. It's still daughter Jan's favorite birthday dinner.

1½ pounds lean top round steak
½ pound boneless pork loin chops (this cut of meat is easy to cut into cubes;
    not to be confused with pork tenderloin).
½ cup extra-virgin olive oil
3 large onions, chopped
5–6 ribs celery, diced
1 can beef bouillon
1 can water
4 tablespoons light soy sauce
1 can bean sprouts, drained
1 can water chestnuts, drained and sliced
8 ounces mushrooms, sliced and sautéed in 1 tablespoon olive oil
2 tablespoons cornstarch
¾ cup water

Pressure cooker: Cut meats into ½ to ¾-inch cubes. In a large skillet, over medium heat, heat oil. Brown meats, preferably in 2 batches. Add to pressure cooker together with onion, celery, bouillon, and water. Deglaze the skillet with water and pour into cooker. Add soy sauce. Bring pressure up to 15 pounds. When this pressure is reached, the pressure regulator will begin to rock. Lower heat, but retain enough to maintain pressure (a gentle rocking of the pressure regulator will tell you this). Let pressure come down (do not cool cooker). Follow directions below for completing dish.

Conventional method: After meat is cooked either in pressure cooker or on stove, add bean sprouts, water chestnuts, and sautéed mushrooms. Adjust seasoning, adding more salt and soy sauce if needed. Mix cornstarch with water and add to mixture, stirring constantly until gravy is thickened. Serve over rice and top with crispy Chinese noodles. Now all you need is a tossed salad, a dessert, and a long walk afterward.

MAKES 6 SERVINGS.

HAM LOAF

Every now and then Jan will call me and say, "Mom, I think it's time for some ham loaf." That's when we head for her kitchen and whip up this tasty loaf and have it for dinner. What you don't eat that night, make into sandwiches for lunch the next day. Mmmm, good!

¾ pound ham
½ pound veal
¼ pound pork
2 eggs, beaten
¾ cup soft bread crumbs
¾ cup milk
Grind of black pepper
2 teaspoons prepared mustard*
¼ cup packed brown sugar*
⅓ cup pineapple juice*

   In a meat grinder, add meats and grind. (I call my butcher and ask him to grind the meats.) In a large bowl, mix in eggs, bread crumbs, milk, and pepper. Pat mixture in 9 x 5 x 3-inch loaf pan. Mix mustard and brown sugar and spread on top of loaf. Pour juice over loaf. Bake at 350 degrees for 1½ hours.

MAKES 6 SERVINGS.

*I often omit the last three ingredients and it's just as good.

HOOSIER CHILI

This recipe appeared in the November 1991 *Country Extra* magazine. It is so near to the chili Mother made that I saved the recipe and have served it many times. It was submitted to the magazine by Jean Boberg, who lives in Muncie, Indiana. When I was compiling my recipes, I got Jean's number through directory information, called her up, and got her permission to print this.

2 pounds extra-lean ground beef
2 cups chopped onion
¾ cup chopped celery
½ cup chopped green bell pepper
3 garlic cloves, minced
1 teaspoon salt
¼ teaspoon black pepper
1 tablespoon brown sugar
3 tablespoons chili powder, or to taste
2 16-ounce cans stewed tomatoes
1 46-ounce can tomato or V8 vegetable juice
1 can beef broth
½ cup uncooked elbow macaroni
1 15-ounce can kidney beans, rinsed and drained

MUNCIE ★

In large Dutch oven or soup kettle, brown beef until no longer pink. Add onions, celery, peppers, and garlic. Continue cooking until vegetables are tender. Add all remaining ingredients except macaroni and beans. Bring to a boil. Reduce heat, cover, and simmer for 1½ hours, adding macaroni for last half hour of cooking time. Stir in beans and heat through.

MAKES 12 SERVINGS (ABOUT 4½ QUARTS).

David's Fried Baloney Sandwich

One evening I got a call from David when he was still doing his show at NBC and he asked me on the air how to make this sandwich. It had always been just about his favorite lunch, but I didn't know how fondly he remembered it until he called me that night.

2 slices white, seven-grain, or oatmeal bread
2 slices baloney

2 slices fresh tomato
Mustard (hot dog variety)

In a small nonstick skillet, heat the baloney slices (do not overcook). Make 1 cut from center to edge of baloney slice so it doesn't cup. Spread 1 slice bread with mustard. Put on the baloney and tomato slices. Top with the other slice of bread. Enjoy!

MAKES 1 SANDWICH.

HOT TUNA SANDWICH

I got this from my daughter Jan years and years ago. One night when David was working as a weatherman here in Indianapolis at Channel 13, I went to pick him up to go to a hockey game. I knew that he didn't have time for dinner before the game, so I fixed a hot tuna sandwich, wrapped it in foil, and took it to him with some green beans and salad. He had a hot meal on the run. It was my first and last hockey game. I've always preferred basketball to hockey, but it was nice to be there with him.

> 1 cup grated sharp cheese
> 1 7-ounce can water-packed tuna, drained and flaked
> 1 tablespoon grated onion
> 1 jalapeño pepper, seeded and chopped
> 2 tablespoons fresh lemon juice
> 1 tablespoon prepared mustard
> ¾ teaspoon salt
> 1 4-ounce container whipped cream cheese
> 4 hamburger buns

In a medium bowl, mix all ingredients thoroughly. Scoop the center out of the buns, and fill with mixture. Wrap in foil and heat at 425 degrees for 15–20 minutes. These sandwiches can be frozen.

MAKES 4 LARGE SANDWICHES.

Meat Loaf, My Mother's Way

This is the old standby, the one I learned from my mother. In recent years I've added the mushroom soup, to make it moist. Mushrooms are good in just about anything.

1½ pounds lean ground beef (90 percent fat-free)
½ pound good pork sausage
1 cup soft bread crumbs
1 egg, well beaten
1 onion, chopped
1 can cream of mushroom soup, diluted with 1 can water
1 teaspoon salt

In a large bowl, mix meats, bread crumbs, egg, and onion. Add half the soup and mix. Add more soup, if needed, for a moist consistency. Add salt. Spread mixture in a 9x5-inch loaf pan and bake at 325 degrees for about 1 hour and 15 minutes. Remove from oven and let stand for 15 minutes before slicing.

MAKES 6 SERVINGS.

MEAT LOAF, GRANDSON BILL'S WAY

This is a new recipe, which was given to me by my grandson, Bill Millholland, Jan's son, who was born in 1970. He lives in New York City, works for CBS, and is getting ready to go to Japan, where he will be involved with the CBS coverage of the 1998 Winter Olympics. He speaks fluent Japanese. He's also fluent in the kitchen.

½ pound ground beef
½ pound ground pork
½ pound ground veal
1 medium onion, chopped
3 medium mushrooms, coarsely chopped
1 egg, well beaten
⅓ cup dry bread crumbs
1 large clove garlic, minced
¼ cup good quality plum sauce (Dynasty or Lee Kum Kee)
A few splashes of Worcestershire sauce
½ cup milk (Grandma's addition)

Preheat oven to 350 degrees. In a large bowl, mix all ingredients together (mixing with hands works best) until well blended (and the different colors of meat are no longer noticeable). Spread mixture into a large bread loaf pan and bake at 375 degress for 50 55 minutes.

MAKES 6 SERVINGS.

Grandson Bill, an opera buff and good guy, in his mother's kitchen, shortly before he moved to New York in 1995. OPPOSITE: My mother, who taught me love of cooking, love of gardening, and love of flowers.

Stuffed Peppers

I always loved bell peppers, although I never got to enjoy them growing up because Dad just couldn't stand them (or mustard, either). But Hans and I both like them so very much that we raise them in our vegetable garden in the backyard. I concocted this recipe myself. Serve a large stuffed pepper with a salad and some crusty bread and you have your meal. These peppers can be prepared very quickly, so I keep some in the freezer year-round and if I think I won't have time to cook the next day, I take them out and put them in the refrigerator so they'll defrost overnight.

1 tablespoon extra-virgin olive oil
1 onion, chopped
1 pound lean ground beef (90 percent fat free)
1 2-cup package boil-in-bag rice, cooked
1 8-ounce can tomato sauce
1 teaspoon salt
4 medium green bell peppers

In a large skillet, over medium heat, heat oil and sauté onion until soft. Add beef and cook until no longer pink, breaking it up into tiny pieces. Add 1½ cups cooked rice (the rest can be put in the freezer for another time). Add tomato sauce and salt. Meanwhile, seed the green peppers and blanch them in boiling water for 5 minutes; drain. Stuff peppers with meat mixture. Either leave them whole or cut in half, lengthwise, if they are large. Put in baking pan with a small amount of water and bake at 350 degrees for 30 minutes. Can be frozen.

Makes 4 servings.

Hint: For a vegetarian meal, peppers can be stuffed with a mixture of sautéed onion, chopped green pepper, rice, and 2 or 3 fresh chopped tomatoes. One pint of stewed tomatoes can also be substituted for fresh tomatoes.

Shish Kebabs

OVERLEAF: **Shish kebabs good enough for a Girl Scout.**

Once my daughter Gretchen's birthday, May 25, fell on the date of her annual Girl Scout camp-out, so I sent her off with her favorite dinner for the whole troop. I included all the skewers and fixings and they assembled the shish kebabs themselves and cooked them over the fire. Her scout leader provided the birthday cake.

MARINADE
2 bay leaves
6 whole black peppercorns, crushed
¾ cup cider vinegar
⅓ cup water
1½ teaspoons sugar

MEAT
2 pounds tenderloin or sirloin tip, cut into 1½-inch cubes
1 small onion, finely chopped
1 large clove garlic, minced

To make marinade: In a small saucepan, bring all ingredients to a boil and let simmer for a couple of minutes. Cool. Put in a jar with 2 tablespoons of olive oil and shake well. In a 2-quart bowl, place meat and sprinkle with onions and garlic. Pour marinade over meat. Cover and let stand in the refrigerator for at least 3–4 hours (overnight is okay).

VEGETABLES
16 cherry tomatoes
16 mushrooms, washed, dried, stems removed
4 medium green bell peppers, cut into 1½-inch squares
4 medium onions, quartered and separated into layers
Salt and pepper

Drain marinade from meat and keep for basting. Slide a piece of meat on skewer, then a tomato, a whole mushroom, a green pepper square, and a layer of onion. Continue to alternate the meat and vegetables in this order, ending with cube of meat. Set skewers over hot coals and baste with marinade, turning several times to brown evenly about 5 minutes. Sprinkle meat with salt and pepper and push onto serving plates with fork.

MAKES 4 SERVINGS.

Uncle Earl's Creamed Chipped Beef on Tater Tots

My brother Earl is a bachelor cook. This is one of his specialties. It can be prepared in a matter of minutes, and when I tested it, I was surprised at how good it actually was. I don't think I'll make it a regular on my menu, though, because Hans says he got enough chipped beef when he was in the army.

1 package Stouffer's frozen creamed chipped beef
1 package Ore-Ida Tater Tots frozen shredded potatoes

Heat chipped beef and Tater Tots according to package directions. Put the creamed chipped beef on heated Tater Tots. Serve with cooked frozen peas and a garden salad.

MAKES 2 SERVINGS.

TENNESSEE MOUNTAINTOP BACON

From the Von-Bryan Inn, a large log house on Hatcher Mountain just outside of Sevierville, Tennessee, and a favorite weekend getaway for Hans and me. I discovered it when it was written up in a magazine and I needed a place to go relax after working on the 1991 church women's bazaar. At the Von-Bryan, we like to sit on the porch and look across the valley to the Great Smoky Mountains. We take hikes over rocks and little streams, and there are beautiful waterfalls to be found everywhere. Jo Ann Vaughn, who owns the inn with her husband, D.J., often serves this bacon for breakfast with scrambled eggs or her wonderful French toast.

½ cup flour
¼ cup packed brown sugar
1 teaspoon black pepper
1 pound country style (thick-sliced) bacon

Mix flour, sugar, and black pepper together and coat bacon. Pan fry or bake in 400-degree oven until brown and crisp.

MAKES 4–6 SERVINGS

VON-BRYAN INN
2402 Hatcher Mountain Road
Sevierville, TN 37862
(615) 453-9832 • (800) 633-1459

SWEDISH MEATBALLS

From Barbara Gaines, David's faithful *Late Show* associate producer. Barbara has been with the show since it was at NBC and is most famous for her appearances as the "How's the Weather Out There" girl. This recipe was given to her by her mother, Sophie.

6 saltines
½ cup water
1 pound ground round beef
1 8-ounce jar grape jelly
1 12-ounce jar chili sauce
juice of 1 lemon
Salt and pepper to taste

To make the meatballs, soften saltines in water and add to the meat. Add salt and pepper and mix well. Form into round balls and refrigerate for ½ hour. In a medium saucepan, combine the grape jelly, chili sauce, and lemon juice. Simmer on low for 10 minutes. Remove meatballs from refrigerator and add to saucepan. Cook over low heat for 20–25 minutes until the meat is browned and cooked through. Serve over rice or noodles.

MAKES 4 SERVINGS.

HOUSE SPECIAL MOTHER'S OVEN-FRIED CHICKEN

Most of Mother's meat dishes consisted of chicken. When I was a girl, my family raised chickens. It was always Dad's job to go out and catch and prepare the chickens, then Mother would dress the bird. I never had any part of that. In the 1950s, Dad left coal mining to go into chicken production full-time, selling fresh country eggs to grocers and to neighbors who knocked on the back door.

The secret weapon here is a good cast-iron skillet. Mother never prepared her oven-fried chicken without it. This is a simple recipe, but oh so scrumptious!

1 3-pound whole fryer, cut into pieces
Flour
Salt and pepper
Vegetable oil

Roll chicken pieces in flour mixed with salt and pepper. Shake off excess flour. In a large cast-iron skillet, over medium heat, heat oil. Add chicken pieces and fry until golden brown, about 10–15 minutes. Cover skillet and transfer to preheated 325-degree oven and let bake for about 35–40 minutes until tender. Meat will fall off the bone.

MAKES 4–6 SERVINGS.

CROCK-POT CONTINENTAL CHICKEN

If you are having guests for dinner and have a busy day, this chicken is wonderful. Serve with a tossed salad, maybe some cranberry jelly and an easy dessert—Red Raspberry Pie (see page 161) or some ice cream and homemade cookies that you have pulled out of the freezer.

1 package dried beef
8 boneless, skinless chicken breasts
8 slices bacon
¼ cup sour cream
¼ cup flour
1 can cream of mushroom soup, undiluted

On bottom of greased Crock-Pot, arrange dried beef. Wrap each piece of chicken with a strip of bacon and lay on top of dried beef. In a small bowl, blend sour cream and flour; add soup and mix thoroughly. Pour mixture over chicken. Cover and cook on low, 8–10 hours (or 3–5 hours on high). Serve over hot buttered noodles.

MAKES 8 SERVINGS.

The Greatest Grocery Store on Earth

You may have seen Atlas Supermarket on David's show. Atlas is located only seven blocks from where we lived. Once when David's Bangladeshi pals Sirajul and Mujibur, who work at the souvenir and T-shirt shop next door to the Ed Sullivan Theater (home to "The Late Show"), came to town to tape some segments, they were taped shopping at Atlas.

  When he was a teenager, David bagged groceries and worked there as a stock boy, and eventually worked his way up to cashier. He got a good business sense from Atlas' owner, Sydney Maurer, and I'm sure he gave Sydney and manager Charlie Davis a few headaches in return. Once, David stacked the can display all the way to the ceiling, so customers couldn't get a can from the stack without bringing the whole thing down on top of them. This drove Charlie crazy. But David thought the world of Charlie. I remember during one winter storm, he went out of his way to give Charlie a ride to work.

  I've been shopping at Atlas since 1945. Minus David's artistic stacking methods, the store has changed very little over the years. Sydney still runs the place with his wife, Eleanor. It's not a great big place, and the aisles are narrow, but Sydney has everything that you could want at Atlas, and if he doesn't have it, he'll order it for you. He's famous for his lean beef tenderloins, and gives the following recipe to his customers when they ask how to prepare it. I've used it for years, and it's never failed me.

OPPOSITE: **Looking over—but never squeezing—the fruit at Atlas.**

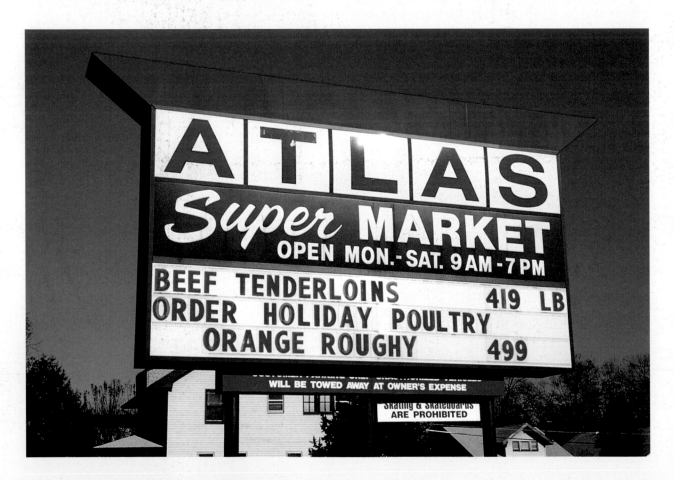

A special tenderloin dinner deserves one of Atlas' beautiful mixed bouquets.

20~20~20~20 TENDERLOIN

3–4 pounds beef tenderloin
3 garlic cloves
2 teaspoons finely minced fresh rosemary
2 teaspoons finely minced fresh thyme

Remove meat from refrigerator. Rub garlic cloves on tenderloin and season (NO SALT) with minced herbs. Allow to sit for 20 minutes. Preheat oven to 475 degrees with broiler pan in oven. Place tenderloin on pan in oven and reduce heat to 375 degrees for 20 minutes. Reduce heat again to 325 degrees for 20 minutes. Remove from oven and tent with foil. Let it "rest" for 20 minutes…then slice.

MAKES 8 SERVINGS.

Bordelaise Mushroom Sauce

Years ago I refined this recipe from various cookbooks. I've had this recipe for years and never served beef tenderloin without it. David didn't spend much time in the kitchen, but he always insisted on preparing the mushroom sauce himself when we had it. He liked the sauce so much, that's why he enjoyed making it. He didn't get to do it very often, though. I only served the sauce with tenderloin, and tenderloin was only for special occasions.

2 tablespoons butter
1 shallot, finely chopped
1 clove garlic, finely chopped
1 onion slice
2 carrot slices
Sprig of parsley
6 whole black peppercorns
1 whole clove
1 bay leaf
2 tablespoons flour
1 cup canned beef bouillon, undiluted
¼ teaspoon salt
⅛ teaspoon black pepper
⅓ cup Burgundy wine
1 tablespoon finely chopped fresh parsley
1 cup thickly sliced mushrooms
1 tablespoon unsalted butter

In a medium skillet, slowly heat butter. Add shallot, garlic, onion and carrot slices, parsley sprig, peppercorns, clove, and bay leaf. Sauté until onion is golden, about 3 minutes. Remove from heat. Add flour, stirring until smooth. Over very low heat, cook, stirring until flour is lightly browned. Remove from heat and stir in bouillon. Over medium heat, bring to boiling point, stirring constantly. Reduce heat, simmer gently, stirring occasionally. Strain. Discard vegetables. Add salt, pepper, Burgundy, and chopped parsley. Meanwhile, in a small skillet, sauté mushrooms in butter, stirring until tender. Add to sauce and reheat gently.

MAKES ABOUT 2 CUPS.

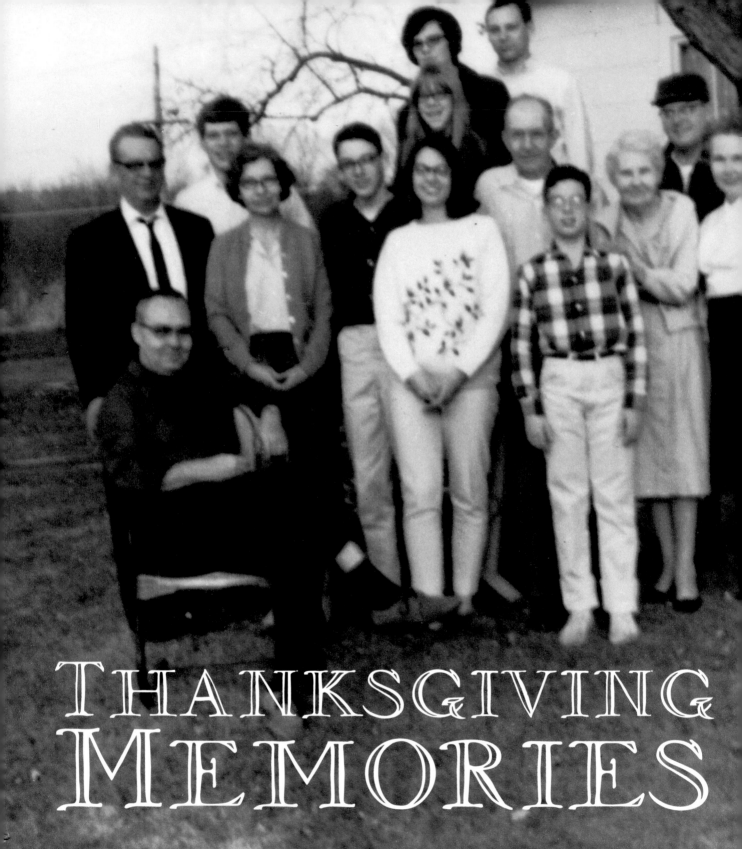

THANKSGIVING
MEMORIES

I grew up lucky. A set of grandparents lived in the houses on either side of us, so we never had to go far to celebrate Thanksgiving. But if not by geography, the maternal and paternal branches of my family tree were tangled up in other ways. Dad's father had died when he was twelve and so Dad's widowed mother, my grandmother, kept food on her table by running a boardinghouse in Des Plaines, Illinois. One of my paternal grandmother's tenants was my maternal uncle, Henry. One thing led to another, and Henry married Grandmother. (Since Henry was the oldest of my mother's six siblings and Grandmother had started her family so early, they weren't that far apart in age.) All this happened before I was born, so when I came into the world, Uncle Henry was also Grandpa Henry. It was a crazy, mixed-up situation. To this day, my kids still can't get it through their heads, but perhaps you can figure it out if you take a look at my Family Tree (see page 104).

Thanksgiving at Grandmother and Grandpa Henry's house always included one thing: goose. All my friends were having turkey at their grandmas', so as a little girl I wasn't comfortable with our having this strange bird. Now, of course, I appreciate how good the goose really was, though I don't know if I would try roasting one myself. I stick to turkey and my family is grateful.

It's funny how Thanksgiving traditions evolve in different families. Since my husband Joe was a florist, he often had to work Thanksgiving morning, delivering people's centerpieces, and he'd come home hungry. So we always had dinner early in the afternoon. That tradition has continued in my home over the years. After dinner, with the family here, we spend the afternoon watching football, napping, or working a jigsaw puzzle, which we spread out on the dining-room table. If anyone's hungry by evening, I put out cold leftover turkey, cold cranberry sauce, and paper plates. By then we've washed enough dishes.

These days Jan, who lives here in Carmel, and I handle Thanksgiving dinner for the family.

The last time I had all the kids here was in 1988, the year that Hans and I moved into our new home, and I insisted they all come that year. But usually it's too much for Gretchen and her husband, Bill, to get here with Liam and Annagrace from Florida for the day, and David always does his show on Thanksgiving night, which keeps him in New York. I suppose I'm lucky to have even one or two of my kids with me on Thanksgiving. We raise our children to let them go and make their own lives, which mine certainly have, so it's okay.

In 1994 I didn't get to spend Thanksgiving with my son, but I did spend it with a *Late Show* camera crew and even a special guest star—Richard Simmons. He came to our home on Wednesday and the crew taped him as he clowned around in the kitchen while I cooked. I baked the stuffing and the pies amid cables and lights and wires. Although it was hectic, it was also fun. At one point, Richard thought it would be funny if we danced, and Hal Gurnee,

Thanksgiving, 1988, the last time I had all my kids together at home. LEFT TO RIGHT: Me, David, Gretchen, and Jan.

Precious cargo for Richard Simmons. He carried this cherry pie back to New York and presented it to David on "The Late Show."

the director who was monitoring all the goings-on from New York, said, "Richard, NO DANCING!" We taped a segment and Richard flew back to New York with a homemade cherry pie. During the show on Thanksgiving night, Richard walked out on stage carrying the cherry pie and presented it to David. It looked as though he had walked right out of my kitchen and onto David's show. Then we did a live hookup from Indianapolis—Jan's family, Uncle Earl, Hans, and I—just before we sat down to have Thanksgiving dinner. On the air, David tried to guess what kinds of pies I had made. It was the next best thing to having him here.

MY FAMILY TREE

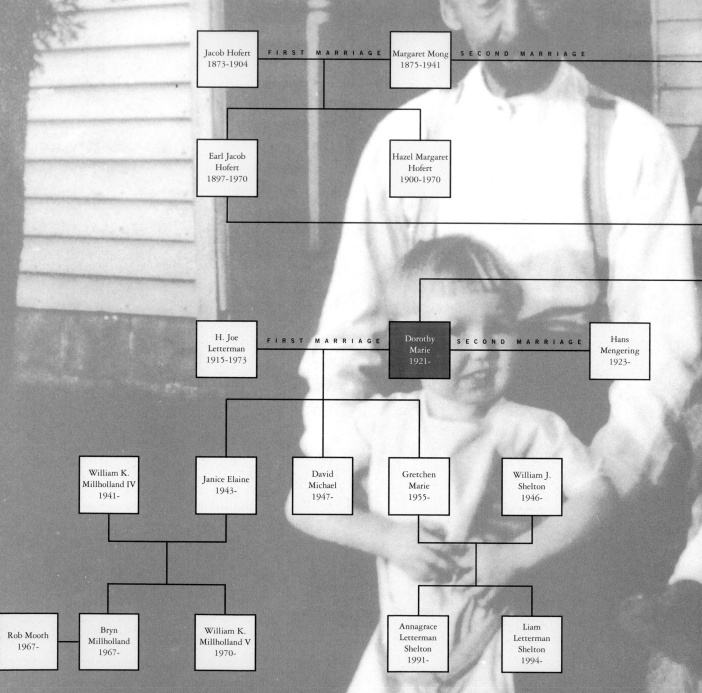

Jacob Hofert
1873-1904

FIRST MARRIAGE

Margaret Mong
1875-1941

SECOND MARRIAGE

Earl Jacob
Hofert
1897-1970

Hazel Margaret
Hofert
1900-1970

H. Joe
Letterman
1915-1973

FIRST MARRIAGE

Dorothy
Marie
1921-

SECOND MARRIAGE

Hans
Mengering
1923-

William K.
Millholland IV
1941-

Janice Elaine
1943-

David
Michael
1947-

Gretchen
Marie
1955-

William J.
Shelton
1946-

Rob Mooth
1967-

Bryn
Millholland
1967-

William K.
Millholland V
1970-

Annagrace
Letterman
Shelton
1991-

Liam
Letterman
Shelton
1994-

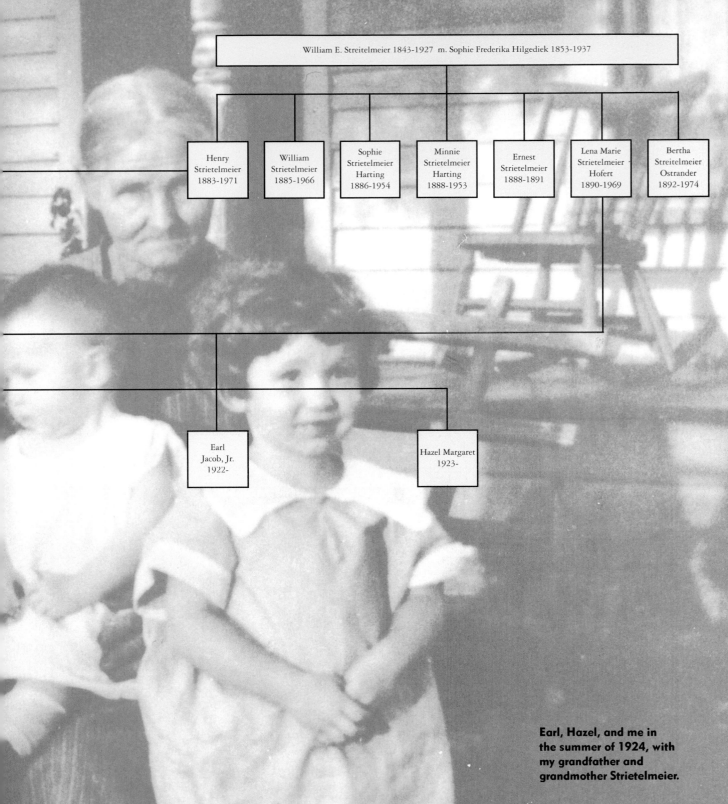

William E. Strietelmeier 1843-1927 m. Sophie Frederika Hilgediek 1853-1937

Henry
Strietelmeier
1883-1971

William
Strietelmeier
1885-1966

Sophie
Strietelmeier
Harting
1886-1954

Minnie
Strietelmeier
Harting
1888-1953

Ernest
Strietelmeier
1888-1891

Lena Marie
Strietelmeier
Hofert
1890-1969

Bertha
Strietelmeier
Ostrander
1892-1974

Earl
Jacob, Jr.
1922-

Hazel Margaret
1923-

**Earl, Hazel, and me in
the summer of 1924, with
my grandfather and
grandmother Strietelmeier.**

LETTERMAN THANKS-GIVING FAVORITES

CRANBERRY GEL

My mother's recipe. We didn't like the whole cranberries, so she whipped up this delicious gel.

4 cups fresh cranberries
1 cup water
2 cups granulated sugar

In medium saucepan, over medium heat, add berries and water. Cook until berries pop, then push through a Foley mill (from Foley Manufacturing Co., Minneapolis, Minnesota). Add sugar and bring to a boil. Keeps well in the refrigerator and is good with most any meat or poultry. The gel can be served in an attractive glass bowl or put in glass jars with straight sides. When chilled it will slide out of jar and can be sliced for serving.

MAKES 4 CUPS.

CRANBERRY SAUCE

From Joe Moore, the present director of food services at Second Presbyterian. He got this hearty sauce from a church member, Jane Faris.

2 cups packed light brown sugar
2 cups granulated sugar
Grated rind of 3 oranges
1 cup orange juice
½ teaspoon ground cinnamon
3 pounds fresh cranberries

In a large saucepan, over medium heat, combine sugars, orange rind, orange juice, and cinnamon. Bring to a boil. Add cranberries, cover and cook until cranberries burst (approximately 4–5 minutes). Refrigerate. The sauce gels when cold.

MAKES 6 CUPS.

Note: Recipe can be halved.

Dicing bread for stuffing. I don't know what my family would do to me if I left stuffing off the Thanksgiving menu.

HOMEMADE APPLESAUCE

I make this applesauce in early July when Lodi or Transparent apples are available, then I store it in the freezer. That way I have a taste of summer all winter long. And, of course, it's always on the Thanksgiving table.

8 large apples, peeled, cored, and quartered
¾ cup water
⅓ cup granulated sugar (or to taste)

In a medium saucepan, cook apples with water until they make a smooth sauce, then stir in sugar. Put in freezer jars.

MAKES 3 PINT JARS.

STUFFING

I prefer to bake stuffing separate from the turkey. Adjust seasonings by tasting it along the way. My daughter Jan always samples my stuffing for me before it is baked to make sure it's going the way it should.

> 1 family-size Pepperidge Farm sandwich bread loaf
> 1 stick unsalted butter
> 3 large onions, chopped
> 6 ribs celery, finely sliced
> Dried sage leaves
> Dried thyme leaves
> 2 cups water
> 1 medium potato, peeled and cut into pieces
> 1 egg
> 1 cup milk
> 1 quart chicken broth

Spread bread slices on a cookie sheet and let air dry for a couple of days, then toast lightly in the oven. Cut in cubes and put in a large mixing bowl. In a small skillet, over medium heat, melt butter and sauté onions and celery. Add to bread. Crumble sage and thyme leaves over bread cubes (begin with 1½ teaspoons of each herb and taste after liquids are added). In a small saucepan, cook potato in 2 cups water until soft. When potato is done, mash it in the water and add to the stuffing mix. Whisk egg in milk and add chicken broth. Stir all together. To test seasonings, and to avoid eating raw egg in mixture, in a small skillet with 1 teaspoon of oil, sauté a spoonful of stuffing. Add more salt, sage, and thyme, if needed. If the stuffing is not moist enough, add more milk and/or chicken broth.

MAKES ENOUGH FOR MY CLAN WITH SOME LEFT OVER.

Hint: After the turkey is done, there will be plenty of broth to add to the stuffing and to make gravy.

OPPOSITE: **David, 6, in the Palm Beach jacket I bought real quick for his kindergarten graduation.**

CREAMED PEAS WITH PEARL ONIONS OR MUSHROOMS

This vegetable combination has stood me in good stead over the years. It's quick and easy to fix and goes well with nearly everything. If you're using pearl onions from the produce department, make sure you skin them according to package directions.

> *2 packages frozen peas*
> *1 package frozen pearl onions, or 1 pint pearl onions, skinned*

In medium saucepan, cook peas according to package directions. In another pan, cook pearl onions until done.

> WHITE SAUCE
> *1 tablespoon unsalted butter*
> *1 tablespoon flour*
> *¼ teaspoon salt*
> *1 cup milk*
> *⅛ teaspoon white pepper*

In small saucepan, melt butter. Blend in flour and salt, stirring until smooth. Gradually stir in milk and white pepper and cook until thickened. Combine peas, onions, and sauce, and serve.

MAKES 8 SERVINGS.

Hint: If you want peas and mushrooms, use either a small can of sliced mushrooms, drained, or sauté fresh sliced mushrooms in a bit of olive oil until tender and add to peas. Omit cream sauce.

Lights, Camera, London

A foggy day in London town. I made my "Late Show" debut in front of Big Ben. Who could ask for a better co-star?

A little less than a year after I made my television debut covering the Winter Olympics for "The Late Show," producer Maria Pope asked me if Hans and I had up-to-date passports. She didn't say any more than that, but I had an inkling that another trip abroad for "The Late Show" was in the works. On April 26, 1995, Hans and I were on our way via the Concorde to London to do remote spots for "The Late Show," which would air from London the week of May 15.

It was my first trip to London, and I got to see a lot of it during our time there, with a camera crew watching me watch the sights. I was taped riding atop a double-decker sightseeing bus, exclaiming, "Wow" at the sight of Stonehenge, and draining a pint of beer at a pub. The bartender filled the glass and set it in front of me, the cameraman cut, we poured out most of the beer, and came back to me finishing off the last bit from the mug. It looked like I drained the whole thing. Oh, goodness!

We spent a week taping spots, then returned to the States. On May 12, we found our way back to London for the week of "The Late Show" broadcasts. The first night we broadcast, I stood across the Thames River from Big Ben and told David when it was about to chime the hour of 6.

The British aren't known for their food, except for their notorious fish and chips, but we did have remarkably good salads there. One night we had dinner at a Lebanese restaurant where there was a bowl filled with sweet, sliced green and red peppers, whole tomatoes, and big leaves of lettuce on the table. There was no dressing or dip for them. We just cut up the vegetables and ate them. They were delicious. Everywhere we went, there were wonderful olives. For breakfast in the hotel dining room, there was a buffet laden with hearty fare. Our favorites were sautéed mushrooms, grilled tomatoes, and scrambled eggs. I've duplicated that a couple of times here at home for Hans and me. It reminds us of London and it makes an excellent breakfast.

While we were on the run taping segments, I tried the bangers, a coarse grind of seasoned sausage sold by street vendors. Frankly, I still like plain old American hot dogs better. I loved the Dover sole, though. It's such a delicate, flaky fish.

One of the best parts of the trip was the final London show. Near the end of that broadcast, David brought me into the studio where the show was being taped, presented me with a huge bouquet of flowers, and thanked me for all my work. He didn't have to thank me. It was all my pleasure. I carried half a dozen gorgeous red roses from that bouquet home with me on the plane and kept them for another week.

David, 2, and Jan, 5, enjoying a wheelbarrow ride. The chauffeur is their Uncle Earl. RIGHT: Joe in an early garden at home in Indianapolis.

VEGETABLES

I was a Depression child, so I ate what was put before me without much whining. There were always plenty of vegetables, because Mother and Dad had a big garden, so Mother canned pints and pints of peas and corn, and quarts of green beans.

Since my hands were small enough to go down into the jars, it was always my job to give them a good scrubbing on canning day every summer. After the jars were washed and filled with whatever vegetable was being canned that day, Mother would place them in a huge copper boiler and boil them for three hours until they were considered sterile and safe. On canning days, it was also my job to fix lunch for my mother and sister and myself. I'd prepare each of us some bacon, a fried egg, a sliced tomato, and a piece of bread and butter.

When I was raising my own family, I gathered our vegetables from our own backyard garden. Jan, David, and Gretchen were all pretty good eaters, although David didn't particularly care for spinach or asparagus. Still, getting them to finish their vegetables was not the chore some mothers face. One thing I never did was try to disguise the vegetables in cheese or lots of butter. I just reminded the

kids that their dessert wouldn't appear until the vegetables disappeared.

Joe died in 1973 and Hans and I were married in 1983. He and I lived for a few years in the Broad Ripple area, in the home where I raised my family. Then, in 1988, we decided to move. We built a three-bedroom house on a quiet cul-de-sac in Carmel. The first order of business was to plant flowers and then create a small vegetable garden in the backyard. Hans takes as much pleasure as I do in tending it. We also have a birdbath with a small heater so it doesn't freeze, and we are visited by robins, cardinals, chickadees, and finches all year long. I keep them coming back by feeding them with pinecones coated in peanut butter and bacon drippings and rolled in birdseed, in addition to several feeders.

We gather a lot of our fresh fruits and vegetables from U-pick farms where we pay to pick produce ourselves. Every summer I still find myself washing jars (now freezer jars), making sure we have enough fruits and vegetables in the freezer to last us year-round. During my last peek in the freezer, I counted sixteen bags of frozen green peas ready and waiting— plus strawberries, raspberries, blueberries, cherries, lima beans, sweet corn, and applesauce.

Buttering Up

A tablespoon of butter or margarine added to cooking peas or lima beans will help keep the pot from boiling over. The lima beans come right over the pan if I don't put some butter or margarine on them.

BROCCOLI LIMA BEAN CASSEROLE

My friend Alma Worthington gave me this recipe about 12 years ago and it's wonderful to have when you need a big dish to take somewhere. I plan to take it to my garden club's spring luncheon. When one of the gals who works out at the fitness center where I exercise heard that I was including it in my book, she said, "I like broccoli, and I like lima beans, but together?" I told her, "You'd be surprised how good it is."

1 10-ounce package frozen chopped broccoli
1 10-ounce package frozen lima beans
1 can reduced-fat cream of mushroom soup
1 package onion soup mix
1 cup light sour cream
1 can water chestnuts, sliced
3 cups Rice Krispies
1 stick unsalted butter

In a medium casserole dish, add broccoli and lima beans. Mix together soups, sour cream, and water chestnuts. Pour on top of vegetable mixture. Cover with Rice Krispies and dot with butter. Bake at 350 degrees for 30 minutes.

MAKES 12 GENEROUS SERVINGS.

HOUSE SPECIAL FOUR-BEAN CASSEROLE

From my niece, Carol Sulanke, sister Hazel's daughter. Carol and her husband, Thom, are both vegetarians, so Carol knows how to make one mean vegetable casserole.

SAUCE
2 tablespoons extra-virgin olive oil
1 medium onion, chopped
4 cloves garlic, chopped
3 tablespoons brown sugar
2 tablespoons cider vinegar
½ cup tomato sauce
1 teaspoon prepared mustard
1 tablespoon chili powder
½ teaspoon liquid smoke

In a small skillet, over medium heat, heat oil and sauté onion and garlic until tender. Add remaining ingredients; stir well.

BEANS
1 15-ounce can baked beans
1 15-ounce can kidney beans, drained
1 15-ounce can black-eyed peas or chick-peas, drained
1 15-ounce can lima beans, drained

In a 2-quart casserole, combine beans and sauce and bake at 350 degrees for 45-60 minutes.

MAKES 8 SERVINGS.

Broccoli Stuffed Tomatoes

I heard about this recipe on a local radio show more years ago than I care to remember and jotted it down. Jan, David, and Gretchen all enjoyed this dish. It's nice to look at and very tasty—a good way to present vegetables to kids.

8 medium tomatoes
1 10-ounce package frozen chopped broccoli
1 cup shredded cheddar cheese
1 cup fine dry bread crumbs
1 small onion, minced
2 tablespoons light mayonnaise
1½ teaspoons salt

Cut each tomato into 5 wedges, leaving connected at base. In a covered saucepan, over medium heat, steam broccoli in ½ cup water for 2 minutes. Drain and combine with remaining ingredients. Spoon equal amounts into each tomato. Press tomato wedges back toward center. Bake in a 325-degree oven on a rack in a shallow pan for 25 minutes.

MAKES 8 SERVINGS.

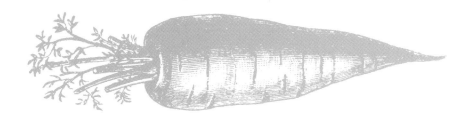

MARINATED CARROTS

Another recipe from my good friend Pat Foster, who serves these carrots as an appetizer, but I think they make a very good salad if you serve them on romaine lettuce. Every time I run across one of Pat's recipes, I can't help but smile. She has a wonderful sense of humor. One day she was grocery shopping and looking at chicken breasts on sale. They were huge and she told the butcher, "But I don't want Dolly Parton chicken." When she later told me this story, I had to laugh.

6–8 carrots, cut into strips
1 small onion, thinly sliced
2 cloves garlic, crushed
1 teaspoon dried basil
1 teaspoon salt
½ teaspoon black pepper
Juice of a large lemon
½ cup extra-virgin olive oil
¼ cup white wine vinegar
Romaine leaves

In a medium saucepan, simmer carrots and onion for 3–5 minutes; drain and put in a medium bowl. In a small bowl, combine seasonings, add vinegar, and stir in oil. Mix well. Pour marinade over carrot-onion mixture. Marinate at least 12 hours in the refrigerator. Drain and serve on romaine leaves.

MAKES 4 SERVINGS.

To Cook or Not to Cook

I like cauliflower and broccoli tender-crisp (al dente), steamed just this side of raw. Brussels sprouts and asparagus are other vegetables that don't need to be cooked to mush. I always thought that peas had to be cooked until they were tender, but at the Country Cook Inn, a homey restaurant near Greentown, Indiana, where Hans and I like to eat (especially on Fridays, for the turkey dinner), the owners, Arlene and Gary Voorhis, put just-defrosted peas on the salad bar. You just put a spoonful of peas onto your salad. Cold or just out of the pod, peas make a really good addition to any salad.

The finer restaurants now cook all their vegetables tender-crisp, so I guess that has become the fashionable way to cook them. Even green beans are often left so crisp you can eat them with your fingers. However, I have always preferred my green beans really tender. I put a pound or so in the pressure cooker with a half cup of water, an onion cut into quarters, and some new potatoes and cook at 15 pounds of pressure for 5 minutes. After the pressure cooker is finished, then I just put in a little bit of fried and diced bacon and the drippings, add salt and pepper to taste, and let them simmer (without pressure) or transfer to a saucepan for 20–30 minutes. I know nutritionists say this takes the nutrients out of the beans, but they taste so good!

ROASTED POTATOES

From Robert Morton, David's executive producer, who has been working with my son since 1982. "Morty" got this recipe from his mother, Sally.

2–3 pounds small red potatoes with skins, scrubbed and quartered
2–3 large onions, quartered
¼ cup extra-virgin olive oil
Salt
Freshly ground black pepper
Dried rosemary
Garlic powder

Preheat oven to 400 degrees. Blot potatoes dry with paper towels. In a mixing bowl, toss potatoes and onions with oil until all the potatoes are coated. Add seasonings. Arrange in a single layer on a baking dish and place in oven. Occasionally shake the pan and turn the potatoes. Bake until golden brown, approximately 40 minutes.

MAKES 6–8 SERVINGS.

SPINACH CASSEROLE

This recipe comes from Carol Jansen, one of my coworkers at Second Presbyterian. It is so delicious that even my brother Earl likes it. He disliked spinach so much as a boy that he put jelly on it to make it go down easier.

1½ tablespoons unsalted butter
1 tablespoon minced onion
4 ounces cream cheese
1½ beef bouillon cubes dissolved in ½ cup hot water
1 egg
1½ cups cooked spinach (1 package frozen), drained well

Combine all ingredients except spinach in blender and process (or beat until it looks like thick milk). In casserole dish, add spinach, then sauce, and stir to blend. Bake at 400 degrees for 20 minutes.

MAKES 3 SERVINGS.

Note: Recipe can be doubled or tripled. You can add a cracker crumb topping, if you desire.

Breads and

BREAKFASTS

Nothing makes the house smell better than cinnamon rolls or muffins baking in the oven. I still remember the smell of sticky buns with brown sugar and hickory nuts baking in Mother's kitchen on Saturdays. She would shoo us away when they were done, though, because she put them aside for Sunday morning breakfast. Oh, how we kids looked forward to those sticky buns! I would often make pancakes for Jan, David, and Gretchen when they were growing up. They also loved biscuits with the cream gravy I would make using bacon drippings, although they wouldn't dare eat anything so fattening and heavy today.

But now I have to shatter some illusions and

Mother and me back home in Linton. I'm only a few months old.

make a confession. I don't think I ever made a plain loaf of homemade bread for my kids. I never learned how from my own mother. I helped her with pies and cakes and things like that, but bread she did on her own. I guess she knew how to do it and just did it herself instead of letting us kids mess it up.

When my children were little, the bread man from Omar Bakery came to the door three days a week. Jan, David, and Gretchen all loved his cupcakes, so sometimes I splurged and bought those, too. They were chocolate with chocolate icing, and filled with cream, like Hostess cupcakes, but these were fresh out of the oven. Now I use a bread maker, which is just a marvelous appliance. I even bought one for both Jan and David. So now, thanks to modern technology, we all have homemade bread any time we want it.

Awesome Orange Chocolate Muffins

Bryn Mooth, my "awesome" firstborn grandchild.

From Bryn Mooth, my first granddaughter, born in 1967. Her favorite word is "awesome." Bryn is married now and living in St. Louis. She learned to cook and to love cooking by helping her mother, Jan, in the kitchen. Every year, on the Saturday after Thanksgiving, Jan, Bryn, and I like to get together in the warmth of Jan's kitchen and start baking our Christmas cookies.

2 cups flour
3 teaspoons baking powder
⅓ cup granulated sugar
½ teaspoon salt
½ cup orange juice
1 teaspoon orange peel
½ cup vegetable oil
½ teaspoon vanilla extract
¼ cup milk
1 egg
¾ cup chocolate chips

Preheat oven to 400 degrees. In a medium bowl, combine dry ingredients and blend with a fork. In a separate bowl, combine liquid ingredients. Gradually pour orange juice mixture into flour mixture, and mix lightly just until flour is moistened. Fold in chocolate chips. Fill lightly greased muffin pans two-thirds full with batter. Bake at 400 degrees for 18–20 minutes.

MAKES 12 MUFFINS.

PUMPKIN MUFFINS

At the Shaker Village (see page 50), these little muffins are always served with breakfast in the main dining room, and they are out of this world. They also come courtesy of Elizabeth Kremer's book, *We Make You Kindly Welcome*.

¾ cup packed brown sugar
¼ cup molasses
½ cup soft unsalted butter
1 egg, beaten
1 cup canned pumpkin
1¾ cups flour
1 teaspoon baking soda
¼ teaspoon salt
¼ cup chopped pecans

In a medium bowl, cream the sugar, molasses, and butter; add egg and pumpkin and blend well. In another bowl, mix the flour with baking soda and salt; beat this mixture into the pumpkin batter. Fold in the pecans. Fill well-greased muffin pans about half full with batter. Bake at 375 degrees for 20 minutes. (They can be frozen until company comes for breakfast.)

MAKES 16 MUFFINS.

BABY FOOD MUFFINS

I know…"*Baby food* muffins?" you might wonder. My longtime friend Virginia Link gave me this recipe years ago. I have made these tasty muffins for my Wednesday morning Bible study group. Needless to say, they have always been a big hit.

1 cup granulated sugar
2 eggs, beaten
½ teaspoon vanilla extract
½ cup vegetable oil
1 junior-size jar plum or applesauce baby food
1 cup unsifted flour
1 teaspoon baking powder
½ teaspoon salt
¼ teaspoon ground cloves
¼ teaspoon ground nutmeg

LEMON GLAZE
½ cup confectioners' sugar
1 tablespoon unsalted butter
1 tablespoon fresh lemon juice

In a medium bowl, combine sugar, eggs, vanilla, oil, and baby food. Beat all together. Add the rest of the ingredients and blend well. Fill lightly greased muffin pans two-thirds full with batter. Bake at 400 degrees for 15–20 minutes. To make glaze, in a small bowl, combine lemon glaze ingredients. Stir until well blended. While muffins are still hot, spoon glaze over muffins.

MAKES 6 MUFFINS.

Egg-cellence

I like my scrambled eggs with a dash of Tabasco sauce, chili sauce, or salsa. Jan, David, and Gretchen also liked mustard on their eggs — poached, scrambled, whatever. I remember how my dad couldn't stand mustard, so we never had it in our house. Once, though, when Gretchen went to visit him and Mother, she asked him for mustard on her eggs, he made a special trip to the grocery store to get a jar of mustard just for her. That's what grandfathers do.

Biff Henderson's Favorite Breakfast

OPPOSITE: **Dad with me in Linton, in front of his prized 1920s Dort automobile.**

Biff is the *Late Show* stage manager, who has been with the show since 1980. I haven't tried his recipe, but it might be good if you like fish for breakfast.

> *1 tablespoon unsalted butter*
> *1 small onion, chopped*
> *1 can chunk light tuna, drained*
> *Salt and pepper*
> *Grits (as much as you want)*
> *Eggs (as many as you want)*

In medium skillet, over medium heat, melt butter and sauté onion. Add tuna to butter mixture. Stir until tuna is heated. Add salt and pepper to taste. Prepare grits and serve as side dish with tuna and any style eggs.

Cheese Grits

From Sally Kerr—a friend of Jan's from Georgia who says, "Not everybody likes plain grits, but everybody loves these. They're great for breakfast, brunch, a picnic, a pitch-in supper, or just about any event. Come to think of it, don't tell people what they're eating until after they've had a chance to enjoy them."

> *4 teaspoons water*
> *½ teaspoon salt*
> *1 cup uncooked regular grits*
> *2 tablespoons unsalted butter*
> *1 pound Velveeta cheese*
> *3 eggs, beaten*
> *Dash of Tabasco sauce or cayenne pepper*

Preheat oven to 350 degrees. In a large saucepan, bring water to a boil. Add salt and gradually stir in grits, cover, reduce heat, and simmer until very thick, stirring occasionally. Add butter, a dash of Tabasco or cayenne pepper, and cheese. Stir until melted. Remove from heat and quickly stir ⅓ cup hot mix into eggs and add egg mixture to remaining hot grits, stirring constantly. Pour into a lightly greased 9 x 12-inch baking dish. Bake for 50 minutes.

MAKES 8–10 SERVINGS.

CHEDDAR CHEESE BISCUITS

Once when granddaughter Bryn was home, she made these yummy cheese biscuits, which she adapted from one of the cooking magazines.

2 cups flour
1 tablespoon granulated sugar
2½ teaspoons baking powder
½ teaspoon salt
1 teaspoon pepper
½ teaspoon baking soda
6 tablespoons chilled unsalted butter, cut into ½-inch pieces
1¼ cups grated extra-sharp cheddar cheese
1 cup (approximately) cold buttermilk

GLAZE
1 egg beaten with 1 tablespoon milk
Poppy seeds

In a medium bowl, combine dry ingredients; cut in butter (use food processor or pastry blender). Mix in cheese. Stir in enough buttermilk to bind dough. Turn onto floured surface and knead gently until combined. Pat out to ¾-inch thickness. Using biscuit cutter, cut into 3-inch rounds. Transfer to ungreased cookie sheet. Brush with glaze and sprinkle with poppy seeds. Bake in 400-degree oven for 18 minutes.

MAKES ABOUT 10 BISCUITS.

BALONEY BREAKFAST

A slice of baloney will "cup" when it is heated on the griddle or in a skillet. Put some scrambled eggs in a baloney cup for a fun breakfast served with fruit or fruit juice and toast.

DEEP-FRIED BISCUITS

I discovered these at the Sherman House, a century-old restaurant and inn in Batesville, Indiana. They're especially good with apple butter. I still remember the first time that we had dinner at this charming establishment. It was 1966, and David had a summer job at a radio station in Greensburg, Indiana, announcing things like births, marriages, hospitalizations, deaths, and women's club meetings. The call letters of the station were WTRE, because there is a tree growing from the tower of the courthouse in Greensburg. When David's stint there ended, Joe, Gretchen, and I drove down to pick him up and then we continued on to Batesville, about 15 miles to the south, for dinner at the Sherman House, complete with Deep-Fried Biscuits.

> 4 cups scalded milk
> 1 envelope active dry yeast
> 5 cups flour
> ½ cup shortening, melted and cooled
> ¼ cup sugar
> 2 teaspoons salt

In a large bowl, add the milk in a stream to the yeast and stir until yeast is dissolved. Beat in 3 cups of the flour and let the batter rise, covered, in a warm place for 1 hour. Then beat in the shortening, sugar, salt, and remaining 2 cups of flour. Beat the dough until it leaves the sides of the bowl and let it rise, covered, in a warm place for 1 hour. Roll out dough ½-inch thick on a lightly floured surface and with a floured 2-inch biscuit cutter, cut out rounds. In a large skillet, in deep, hot oil (350 degrees), fry the rounds in batches, turning them until they are golden brown. Transfer biscuits to paper towels to drain. Serve hot.

MAKES ABOUT 24 BISCUITS.

JUDY'S BREAKFAST CASSEROLE

Joanne Warmoth, who manages a beautiful bed-and-breakfast called the Teetor House in Hagerstown, Indiana, got this recipe from a friend of hers named Judy Dehart, and it has become a Teetor House Specialty. Hans and I like to drive over to Hagerstown a couple of times a year. Teetor House was built as a private residence in 1934 by the blind automobile tycoon Ralph Teetor, who's credited with inventing cruise control in the 1950s.

THE TEETOR HOUSE
Hagerstown, IN

1 2-pound bag Ore-Ida hash brown potatoes, thawed
½ teaspoon salt
½ pound mild sausage
1 small onion, chopped
½ pound shredded Swiss cheese
5 eggs
1 13-ounce can evaporated milk
¼ teaspoon black pepper
½ teaspoon ground nutmeg

Grease a 9x13-inch baking dish. Press potatoes in the bottom and on sides. Sprinkle with salt and brown lightly in the oven. In a medium skillet, brown sausage and onion and drain. Spread over potato crust. Sprinkle with cheese. In another bowl, beat together remaining ingredients and pour onto the crust. Bake at 425 degrees (400 degrees if using a glass dish) for 20–25 minutes.

MAKES 10 SERVINGS.

SOUTHERN SPOON BREAD

A specialty of the Boone Tavern Hotel in Berea, Kentucky. Service in the restaurant and hotel is provided by students at Berea College, which gives work and education to Appalachian students. (Instead of tipping, you can make a donation to the student fund.) The students come around with their pans of hot spoon bread and ask if you want some. Guess what? I never refuse.

3 cups milk
1¼ cups white cornmeal
3 eggs, well beaten
1 teaspoon salt
1¾ teaspoons baking powder
2 tablespoons unsalted butter, melted

In a medium saucepan, bring milk to a rapid boil and stir in cornmeal. Cook until very thick, stirring constantly, to prevent scorching. Remove from heat and allow to cool. When cold, the mixture will be very stiff. Add eggs, salt, baking powder, and melted butter. Beat with an electric mixer for 15 minutes. If a hand beater is used, break the hardened cooked meal into the beaten eggs in small amounts until all is well mixed. Then beat thoroughly for 10 minutes using a wooden spoon. Pour into 2 well-greased casseroles. Bake at 375 degrees for 30 minutes. Serve from casserole by spoonfuls.

Hint: For a true southern flavor, be sure to use white cornmeal.

Rum Buns

Bina Wells, the wife of Second Presbyterian's former business administrator and parish minister, Mac, contributed these buns to my collection.

1 stick unsalted butter
½ cup granulated sugar
¼ cup rum
1 package Pepperidge Farm party rolls (20), 1½-inch square

In a medium saucepan, melt butter, dissolve sugar, and add rum. Blend. Pour over party rolls, cover tightly with foil, and refrigerate overnight. Warm in 325-degree oven for 25 minutes.

MAKES 20 BUNS.

House Special Spinach~Pumpkin Seed Pesto

From Steve Coakley, executive chef at Henry's at the Strater in Durango, Colorado. At Henry's, this spread is served on fresh-baked rolls. But the spread is so good, you can eat it on anything.

1 cup tightly packed spinach
1 cup tightly packed fresh basil
½ cup capers, with juice
¼ cup fresh lemon juice
1 teaspoon finely chopped garlic
1 shallot, finely chopped
1 teaspoon dry mustard
2 teaspoons black pepper
1 cup pumpkin seeds
2 cups vegetable oil
Salt

In food processor or blender, combine spinach, basil, capers, lemon juice, garlic, and shallot; purée until smooth. Add mustard, black pepper, and pumpkin seeds. Add oil slowly to emulsify. Salt to taste.

MAKES 4 CUPS.

ZUCCHINI BREAD

One of my all-purpose standbys. I can take it anywhere. I use small loaf pans that make 4 loaves at a time. In 1995, I was able to put 28 loaves in the freezer (it was a good year for zucchini). Having this bread in my freezer always comes in handy when I don't have time to bake.

2½ cups flour
¼ teaspoon baking powder
2 teaspoons baking soda
1 teaspoon salt
2 teaspoons ground cinnamon
3 eggs
1 cup vegetable oil
2 cups granulated sugar
2 teaspoons vanilla extract
2 cups grated zucchini
1 cup chopped nuts

In a medium bowl, sift together the flour, baking powder, baking soda, salt, and cinnamon. Set aside. In a large bowl, add eggs, oil, sugar, and vanilla. Beat well. Add zucchini, dry ingredients, and nuts. Mix well. Grease and flour pans. Bake at 325 degrees for approximately 50 minutes in four 7½ x 3¾ x 2¼-inch pans, or in two loaf pans, for 65–75 minutes.

MAKES 2–4 LOAVES.

SUGARPLUM LOAF

Another recipe from my friend Virginia Link, who gave it to me several years ago. Because I don't like fruitcake, this makes a nice festive treat at Christmastime.

1¼ cups granulated sugar
¾ cup unsalted butter or margarine
4 eggs
¾ cup buttermilk
1 teaspoon orange extract
1 tablespoon fresh lemon juice
1 3½-ounce can flaked coconut
1 8-ounce package dates, chopped
1 cup chopped orange slice candy
1½ cups chopped pecans
4 cups flour
1 teaspoon baking soda
¼ teaspoon salt

GLAZE
1 cup confectioners' sugar
½ teaspoon orange extract
2–3 tablespoons orange rind

In a large bowl, cream sugar, butter, and eggs until fluffy. Add buttermilk, orange extract, and lemon juice. Blend well. In a small bowl, combine coconut, dates, candy, and pecans. Set aside. In another bowl, sift flour, baking soda, and salt. Combine flour and fruit mixture, mixing well. Stir into creamed mixture. Line bottom of two 9 x 5 x 3-inch loaf pans with waxed paper. Grease waxed paper and sides of pans. Bake at 300 degrees for 1 hour and 50 minutes. To make glaze: In a small bowl, combine sugar, orange extract, and rind. Punch holes in tops of loaves with a toothpick. Remove from pans and drizzle with glaze.

MAKES 2 LOAVES.

ABOVE: **Hans' and my 1995 Christmas tree, surrounded by Hans' 1928 Lionel model train.** OPPOSITE: **Sugarplum loaf, shown with the commemorative Olympic dishes that David bought for me after I went to Lillehammer.**

Jan's first birthday picture. Looks like she's ready for some cake!

I was raised to believe that no meal is complete without dessert. Mother made lots of pies and when Dad headed off to work in the morning, she always made sure he had a small pie—usually one of her wonderful fruit pies—to take in his lunch box.

She also made outstanding lemon meringue and butterscotch pies. But most often, after we had our supper, there was homemade pudding waiting. She could mix up eggs, sugar, and cocoa and milk and make the most delicious chocolate pudding.

By the time I had my own family, there were pudding mixes, so I depended on those when I needed to make a quick dessert. I would serve pudding in a dish with just a dollop of whipped cream on top. When my kids were young, our milk was delivered in bottles with cream standing on top of the milk, so I never had to buy whipping cream at the grocery store. I would simply pour off the cream and whip it.

I still make desserts as often as I can for my kids, even though they're grown now. I send cookies to Gretchen in Florida, and although Jan is a wonderful cook, she doesn't specialize in desserts, so I can still enjoy baking for her. On David's birthday, I send him a pie by overnight express. I know he appreciates that as much as anything I could do for him.

BLUEBERRY PIE

There's never a shortage of blueberries in our house. I think right now I have about 26 pints of blueberries in the freezer, waiting to be turned into pies or just thawed and served over ice cream for dessert or on our morning cereal. Hans and I go up to northern Indiana every summer to pick blueberries. Nothing can compare to northern Indiana blueberries. At the farm Hans and I visit, we pick them ourselves and pay about 99 cents a pound. It's a lot less expensive than buying in the grocery store, and the berries are much, much better.

PIE DOUGH FOR 2-CRUST PIE (SEE PAGE 150)
⅔ cup granulated sugar
¼ cup flour
4 cups blueberries
Unsalted butter
Dash of salt
1 tablespoon fresh lemon juice

In bottom crust, spread mixture of ¼ cup sugar and 2 tablespoons flour evenly. Add berries and remaining sugar and flour. Dot with butter. Sprinkle a dash of salt and the lemon juice over all. Cover with top crust and turn edges under the bottom crust and crimp to seal. Cut slits in top of crust. Sprinkle with a little sugar. Bake at 450 degrees for 20 minutes. Finish baking at 350 degrees for about 30 minutes. To prevent crust from becoming too dark, cover the edges with foil when you turn oven down.

CARROT CAKE

When I was working at the church we had staff meetings every Tuesday morning. When one of the professional staff had a birthday it was up to his or her secretary to provide a "goodie" for him/her to share. I liked to bake a carrot cake. The recipe was submitted by Dorothy Townsend from *Thou Shalt Season With*, Women's Association, Second Presbyterian Church, Indianapolis (1985).

 2 cups granulated sugar
 1½ cups vegetable oil
 4 eggs
 2 cups sifted flour
 1 teaspoon ground cinnamon
 1 teaspoon salt
 2 teaspoons baking soda
 3 cups grated carrots

In a large bowl, and using an electric mixer, combine sugar and oil. Add eggs and beat. Mix in flour sifted with cinnamon, salt, and soda. Fold in carrots. Pour into a 9 x 13-inch greased and floured pan. Bake at 350 degrees for about 45–50 minutes.

 FROSTING
 1 8-ounce package cream cheese
 1 stick unsalted butter
 2 teaspoons vanilla extract
 1 pound box confectioners' sugar

In a medium bowl, cream the cheese, butter, and vanilla. Add sugar and blend until smooth.

CHILLED PERSIMMON PUDDING

Mother never made persimmon pudding, but she turned me on to persimmons when I was just a little girl. There was a wonderful persimmon tree about a mile and a half away from our house and she would take us kids persimmon picking every fall, when the fruit was ripe enough to eat. They're not ripe until they've fallen from the tree, so we'd take them right off the ground. Make sure that they're ripe enough. Otherwise, you just pucker up until you can't stand it. Persimmons have so many seeds that they're difficult to eat. That's why I like them in puddings better, although it does take a while to run them through a sieve to eliminate the seeds. I buy persimmon pulp from the grocer's freezer case for use in puddings. Since the pulp may not be a popular product outside of the Midwest, check with your supermarket or gourmet food shops or ask them if they will order it for you.

> *16 marshmallows, cut into 6–8 pieces (or miniatures)*
> *12 graham crackers, rolled fine*
> *1 pint persimmon pulp (very ripe fruit)*
> *¼ cup granulated sugar*
> *1 cup chopped walnuts*

In a medium bowl, combine all ingredients. Mix well and shape into a log. Wrap in waxed paper and chill for 4 hours or overnight. Slice into servings. This is very rich so keep servings small. Serve topped with sweetened whipped cream.

MAKES 12–16 SERVINGS.

CUP CUSTARDS

This is wonderfully smooth "comfort food." As fattening as they sound, you're not getting that many fattening ingredients considering the number of cups this recipe makes. Plus, I use skim milk, and the custard is as good that way as with whipping cream. Mother taught me how to make cup custards, but she always had a problem with the custard becoming watery and separating. After I was married, I found a foolproof method of preparing the custard by reading various women's magazines, which I have incorporated here into Mother's recipe.

3 eggs
Dash of salt
3 tablespoons granulated sugar
1 teaspoon vanilla extract
3 cups skim milk
Fresh grated nutmeg

In a medium bowl, beat the eggs and a dash of salt with a fork very slightly, just until blended. Add the sugar and vanilla. In a medium saucepan, scald milk (heat just until a skin begins to form on top). Stir into egg mixture; pour into a sieve and strain into 6 custard cups. Grate nutmeg on top. Set in pan of hot water and bake at 350 degrees for approximately 30–35 minutes. Immediately upon removing custard from oven, put cups into a pan of cold water to cool quickly. Chill and serve.

MAKES 6 CUSTARD CUPS.

Coca-Cola Cake

This delightful confection is from my friend Sally Kerr. It has all the ingredients for a sinfully good cake.

2 cups granulated sugar
2 cups all-purpose flour
1 1/2 cups miniature marshmallows
1/2 cup unsalted butter
1/2 cup vegetable oil
3 tablespoons cocoa
1 cup Coca-Cola
1/2 cup buttermilk
1 teaspoon baking soda
2 eggs
1 teaspoon vanilla extract

Preheat oven to 350 degrees. In medium bowl, sift together sugar and flour; add marshmallows. Set aside. In a medium saucepan, over medium heat, add butter, oil, cocoa, and Coca-Cola and bring to a boil. Remove from heat. Pour over dry ingredients and blend well. Add buttermilk, baking soda, eggs, and vanilla. Mix well. Pour into well-greased 9 x 13-inch baking pan. Bake for 45 minutes. Remove from oven and frost immediately.

FROSTING
1/2 cup unsalted butter
3 tablespoons cocoa
6 tablespoons Coca-Cola
1 pound box confectioners' sugar
1 teaspoon vanilla extract
1 cup chopped pecans

In a medium saucepan, over medium heat, combine butter, cocoa, and Coca-Cola. Bring to a boil and add sugar. Remove from heat. Blend well. Add vanilla and pecans.

Flaky Pie Crust

The fat content in a fruit pie comes from the pie crust, and there's just no way to avoid it. I don't think you can make a crust without the fat. I discovered this recipe several years ago in "Thou Shalt Season With." It's one of the best pie crusts I've ever come across.

$^3/_4$ cup shortening
2 cups flour
1 tablespoon granulated sugar
1 teaspoon salt
1 egg yolk
$^1/_4$ cup cold milk
1 tablespoon fresh lemon juice

In a medium bowl, cut shortening into flour, sugar, and salt until the mix looks like cornmeal or small peas. In another bowl, slightly beat egg yolk and combine with milk and lemon juice. Add to flour mixture and mix by hand until it forms a ball. Roll on well-floured pastry cloth with well-floured rolling pin. This pastry maintains its flaky qualities even after being rolled out a number of times.

MAKES PASTRY FOR 1 2-CRUST PIE OR 2 SINGLE-CRUST PIES.

Mother and Dad with, from left to right, Hazel, me, and Earl.

MOTHER'S FLOAT

One of my mother's standards. It's called a float because lumps of meringue "float" on top of the pudding. I loved it when I was a little girl and my kids loved it, too. Pudding is the basis of this dessert.

1 scant tablespoon flour
½ cup granulated sugar
Pinch of salt
1 tablespoon unsalted butter
1 egg, separated
2 cups milk
1 teaspoon lemon extract
1 tablespoon granulated sugar
½ teaspoon vanilla extract

In a small saucepan, combine flour, ½ cup sugar, salt, butter, egg yolk, and milk. Over medium heat bring to a boil. Add lemon extract. Set aside to cool slightly. In a small bowl, beat the egg white until stiff. Fold half the egg white into the pudding mixture. To the remaining beaten egg white, add 1 tablespoon sugar and vanilla extract. Pour pudding into small casserole dish. With a teaspoon, drop lumps of beaten egg white on pudding and brown in 350-degree oven for 5–10 minutes (depending on your oven). Chill and serve.

MAKES 4 SERVINGS.

FRENCH LEMON BARS

My friend Rita Crear, who was a great cook, gave me this recipe. She used to volunteer answering phones at Second Presbyterian one day a week. We always looked forward to seeing her, because she would often bring in treats. She eventually moved away and I lost touch with her. A few years ago word came from her niece in Chicago that Rita had died. I wrote to tell her how fond I was of Rita and how I thought of her every time I made these lemon bars. They were Rita's favorite and now they are my favorite, too.

CRUST
1½ cups flour
⅓ cup confectioners' sugar
¾ cup unsalted butter

In a medium bowl, mix thoroughly. Pat mixture into 9 x 9-inch pan. Bake at 350 degrees for 25 minutes.

FILLING
3 eggs
1½ cups granulated sugar
1 tablespoon flour
3 tablespoons fresh lemon juice
Confectioners' sugar

In a medium bowl, beat eggs well. Set aside. In a medium bowl, sift sugar and flour, and add to eggs. Stir in lemon juice. Pour over butter crust and bake at 350 degrees for another 20 minutes. After removing from oven, dust with confectioners' sugar. Cut into squares.

MAKES 16 SQUARES.

FRESH FRUIT COBBLER

This delightful cobbler was made for me by Mrs. Marsh, a dear elderly lady who used to baby-sit the kids after Joe bought his own flower shop in the early '50s. One night I came home and she and the kids had put this cobbler together. When I have some blackberries in the freezer that need to be used, I'll use them, and if I don't have enough blackberries, I'll throw in some raspberries to supplement. This cobbler can be made with any fresh fruit you have on hand, and it's always good.

FRUIT MIXTURE
⅔ cup granulated sugar
2 tablespoons flour
3 cups fresh fruit (peaches, cherries, blackberries, raspberries, strawberries, or plums)
2 tablespoons unsalted butter

TOPPING
1 cup flour
2 tablespoons granulated sugar
1½ teaspoons baking powder
½ teaspoon salt
⅓ cup shortening
3 tablespoons milk
1 egg
Heavy cream, whipped

In a small bowl, mix sugar and flour. In an 8- or 9-inch nonstick baking dish, layer the fruit. Sprinkle sugar and flour mixture on top. Dot with butter. Set aside. In a medium bowl, sift flour, baking powder, and salt. Add sugar, then shortening, milk, and egg, and stir with a fork until thoroughly blended. Drop by spoonfuls on fruit. Bake at 350 degrees for 25–30 minutes. Serve warm with whipped cream.

MAKES 8 SERVINGS.

Note: If using peaches, add ½ teaspoon of cinnamon and mix. And, if using strawberries, combine with cherries for a yummy result.

Grammy's Broken Glass Torte

When I asked Caissie St. Onge, one of David's assistants at *The Late Show*, to send me a recipe for the cookbook, she told me apologetically that all she could think to send was this Jell-O dessert, which her grandmother had passed down to Caissie's mother. I said, "That's OK, Caissie, lots of people eat Jell-O. Send it along!" I tried this recipe and shared it with friends, who all pronounced it delicious. It's also very pretty, and would be nice to take to a church pitch-in supper, a family reunion, or something like that.

3 packages different flavored Jell-O, and 1½ cups boiling water per package
1 package unflavored gelatin
¼ cup cold water
1 cup pineapple juice
24 graham cracker squares
1 cup granulated sugar, divided in half
½ cup unsalted butter or margarine, melted (no blend)
1 pint heavy cream
1 teaspoon vanilla extract

Prepare each flavor of Jell-O individually, according to package directions, and let them set. (Loaf pans are ideal for this.) Dissolve unflavored gelatin in cold water. Heat pineapple juice on stove top or in microwave. Add hot juice to dissolved gelatin and set aside to cool. Crush graham cracker squares and mix with ½ cup sugar and the melted butter or margarine. Reserve 2 tablespoons of mixture and press the remainder into the bottom of a 13 x 9 x 2-inch pan or baking dish. In a medium bowl, beat heavy cream with mixer on high, adding other ½ cup of sugar and vanilla extract, until soft peaks are formed. Gently fold in the cooled pineapple mixture. Cut the set Jell-O into ½-inch cubes and carefully stir all three flavors into the whipped cream/pineapple mixture. Pour into prepared pan. Sprinkle 2 tablespoons of crust mixture on top. Chill overnight or as long as possible before serving.

KEY LIME PIE IN NO-ROLL CRUST

I asked Gretchen to send along one of her recipes for my book, and this is the one she chose. What else but a key lime pie from sunny Florida?

NO-ROLL PIE CRUST
1½ cups flour
1½ teaspoons granulated sugar
½ teaspoon salt
2 tablespoons cold milk
½ cup vegetable oil (to reduce saturated fat use ½ cup canola oil)

In a pie plate, sift dry ingredients. In a measuring cup, measure milk into oil and whip with a fork. Pour into flour mixture and mix with a fork; pat into place. Bake at 375 degrees for 8 minutes or until golden.

KEY LIME PIE FILLING
1 can sweetened condensed milk
4 eggs, separated
½ cup fresh key lime juice
6 tablespoons granulated sugar
½ teaspoon cream of tartar

In a medium bowl, combine milk, egg yolks, and lime juice. In a small bowl, beat until stiff one egg white; fold into egg mixture. Add to baked pie shell. In a small bowl, beat 3 egg whites and gradually add sugar and cream of tartar. Top filling with meringue and bake in 400-degree oven until golden, approximately 8–10 minutes.

Note: Oven temperatures vary. To be sure the egg yolks are cooked, you might want to bake pie in 325-degree oven for 20 minutes or until the meringue is golden.

Lemon Fluff

From Steve Smith, my personal trainer at the fitness center. That's right, my personal trainer. Jan had been going to him for about a year, and she thought it might be a good thing for Mom to do. Now I go to Steve three times a week (Hans goes twice) for aerobics and workouts with weights. My doctor thinks it's a wonderful idea. Steve instructs us about our fitness goals and diets so it came as a surprise when I asked him for a recipe for my book and he gave me this high-calorie dessert! But I'm very pleased to have it. I made it myself and it's oh, so good!

> 3 eggs, separated
> 1/4 cup fresh lemon juice
> 1/8 teaspoon salt
> 1/2 cup granulated sugar
> Grated rind of lemon
> 1 cup heavy cream
> 1 cup crushed vanilla cookie crumbs

In a medium bowl, beat egg yolks. Add lemon juice, salt, sugar, and rind and beat well. In a double boiler, add mixture and cook until thickened, stirring constantly. Cool. In a small bowl, beat egg whites until stiff peaks form. In another bowl, beat heavy cream and fold into beaten egg whites. Fold whipped mixture into lemon mixture. Put 1/2 cup crushed vanilla cookie crumbs on bottom of 9 x 9-inch baking dish. Pour lemon mixture over crumbs and sprinkle the other 1/2 cup of crushed crumbs on top. Cover with aluminum foil and freeze overnight. Cut into squares and serve.

MAKES 8 SERVINGS.

Lemon Pudding Cake

This recipe is one of daughter Gretchen's favorite desserts. It can be served from a casserole dish or in individual custard cups.

> 2 eggs, separated
> 2/3 cup milk
> 1 teaspoon grated lemon rind
> 1/4 cup fresh lemon juice
> 1/4 cup all-purpose flour
> 1 cup granulated sugar
> 1/4 teaspoon salt

Preheat oven to 350 degrees. In a small bowl, beat egg whites until stiff peaks form. Set aside. In another bowl, beat egg yolks slightly. Add milk, lemon rind, and lemon juice, and beat into egg yolks. In a medium bowl, sift flour, sugar, and salt and add to egg yolk mixture, beating until smooth. Fold into egg whites and pour into ungreased, 1-quart casserole or into 6 custard cups. Place casserole or custard cups in a deep pan on oven rack and pour very hot water 1 inch deep into pan. Bake until golden brown, 45–50 minutes. Serve warm or cold. Custard cups can be unmolded upside down for single servings.

MAKES 6 SERVINGS.

NUT BROWNIES

One of David's favorites, and one of my oldest, most reliable recipes. They're always good to take to friends or whip up for company.

½ cup unsalted butter
½ cup each granulated sugar and corn syrup, or ⅓ cup honey and ⅔ cup corn syrup
2 eggs
6 tablespoons cocoa
1 teaspoon vanilla extract
1 cup flour
¼ teaspoon salt
1 teaspoon baking powder
½ cup nuts (I prefer pecans)

In a large bowl, combine butter, sugar, and corn syrup or honey and beat well. Add eggs one at a time and beat well after each addition. Continue beating until batter becomes light and fluffy. Stir in cocoa and vanilla extract and beat again. In a medium bowl, sift dry ingredients together and blend into cocoa mix. Add nuts to batter. Pour into greased 8 x 12 x 2-inch baking dish. Bake at 350 degrees for 30–40 minutes. Cut while warm and cool on rack.

MAKES 20 SQUARES.

PECAN MOLASSES PIE

My sister Hazel's mother-in-law passed along this recipe to me at the beginning of World War II, when sugar and syrup were hard to come by. If you had a bottle of Karo syrup in your cupboard, you were lucky. It's the first pecan pie recipe I ever had, and it's still the best. I have some hickory nuts drying in the basement, which Hans will crack when they're ready (that's one of Hans' winter jobs—cracking nuts), and I plan to use hickory nuts with this recipe. I think it will be wonderful.

1 9-inch unbaked pie shell (see page 150)
2 tablespoons unsalted butter
½ cup granulated sugar
2 tablespoons flour
¼ teaspoon salt
2 eggs, beaten
1 cup white corn syrup
1 teaspoon almond extract
1 cup broken pecan meats or hickory nuts

In a medium bowl, cream butter and sugar. Add flour and salt and mix well. Add beaten eggs, corn syrup, almond extract, and nuts. Pour into pie shell and bake at 350 degrees for 45 minutes.

RED RASPBERRY PIE

My raspberry pie made its television debut in the summer of 1995. David sent
George Clark, maintenance engineer for the Ed Sullivan Theater, home of *The Late
Show*, to find the best sweet corn in the Midwest. His search finally ended at my
house and *The Late Show* sent a camera crew to shoot us having corn in the backyard.
They wanted to show burgers on the grill and a table set up in the backyard like a
picnic, with ketchup, mustard, and sliced onions, and have George and me sitting at
the table. I added the raspberry pie. With all the crew there, the pie disappeared so
fast that Hans and I didn't get any. That was okay. I can make one for us anytime.

1 graham cracker pie crust (store-bought ones are very good)
1 tablespoon unflavored gelatin
3 tablespoons cold water
1½ cups crushed red raspberries
½ cup granulated sugar
1½ tablespoons lemon juice
Dash of salt
½ cup heavy cream, whipped
Raspberries for garnish

In a small bowl, soften gelatin in cold water; dissolve over hot water. In a medium
bowl, combine raspberries, sugar, lemon juice, and salt. Blend in dissolved gelatin.
Chill until partially set. Fold in whipped cream and pour into crust. Chill until firm.
Serve topped with more whipped cream, if desired, and garnish with whole raspberries.

UPSIDE-DOWN DATE PUDDING

This recipe came from my sister, Hazel, who kept it from Mother's recipe collection. Mother made this often when she had to have refreshments for clubs or Sunday school.

Me, Earl, and Hazel during the summer of 1994.

1½ cups packed brown sugar
1 tablespoon unsalted butter
1½ cups boiling water
1 8-ounce package pitted dates, cut into pieces
1 cup boiling water
½ cup packed brown sugar
2 tablespoons unsalted butter
1 egg, beaten
1½ cups flour
1 teaspoon baking soda
½ teaspoon baking powder
½ teaspoon salt
1½ teaspoons ground cinnamon
1 teaspoon ground nutmeg
Whipped cream for topping

In medium saucepan, over medium heat, combine 1½ cups brown sugar and 1 tablespoon butter into boiling water. Stir until sugar is dissolved. Set this brown sauce aside. In a small bowl, combine dates and boiling water. Set aside. In another small bowl, blend ½ cup sugar, 2 tablespoons butter, and egg. In another bowl, sift together all the remaining dry ingredients. Add to egg-sugar mixture alternately with cooled date mixture. Pour batter into an 8 x 12 x 2-inch baking dish. Pour brown sugar sauce evenly over batter. Bake at 350 degrees for 30 minutes or until cake springs back when touched. Cut into squares. Use spatula to invert onto plates. Serve with whipped cream.

MAKES 16 SERVINGS.

HOUSE SPECIALS

Two blue-ribbon-winning pies from my niece, Carol Sulanke. In the late
1980s and early 1990s, Carol entered her wonderful pies and baked goods in
both the Indiana State Fair and the Monroe County Fair. Her entries won
numerous blue ribbons, including a championship ribbon. During the last few
years she and Thom, her husband, have made a hobby of riding trains, especially steam trains, all across the country. They logged 18,000 rail miles in
1995! Now she doesn't have time to bake entries for fairs, which must make
all the other contestants very happy.

**Hans and me touring
with my niece, Carol
Boughman Sulanke,
and her husband,
Thom on a train trip in
1995. The engine is
the Union Pacific
Challenger #3985.
This is the largest
steam engine still run-
ning.**

BUTTERSCOTCH COCONUT PECAN PIE

2 tablespoons brown sugar
2 tablespoons granulated sugar
3 tablespoons softened unsalted butter
¼ teaspoon salt
2 eggs, slightly beaten
1 12-ounce jar butterscotch ice cream topping
1 teaspoon vanilla extract
½ cup shredded coconut
½ cup chopped pecan halves
1 unbaked 9-inch pie shell

In a medium bowl, combine all ingredients in listed order, stirring after each addition. Pour batter into pie shell. Bake at 350 degrees for 40–45 minutes. Serve at room temperature.

MILLIONAIRE'S PIE (SO RICH)

1 unbaked 9-inch pie shell (see page 150)
¼ cup softened unsalted butter
⅓ cup granulated sugar
2 tablespoons flour
⅛ teaspoon salt
2 eggs, beaten
1 cup white corn syrup
1 teaspoon vanilla extract
½ cup coarsely chopped pecans
⅓ cup shredded coconut
¼ cup miniature chocolate chips

In medium bowl, cream butter and sugar. Add flour and salt; mix well. Beat in eggs, a little at a time, to keep mixture smooth. Add syrup and vanilla. Stir in pecans, coconut, and chocolate chips. Pour into unbaked pie shell; bake at 350 degrees for 45–50 minutes.

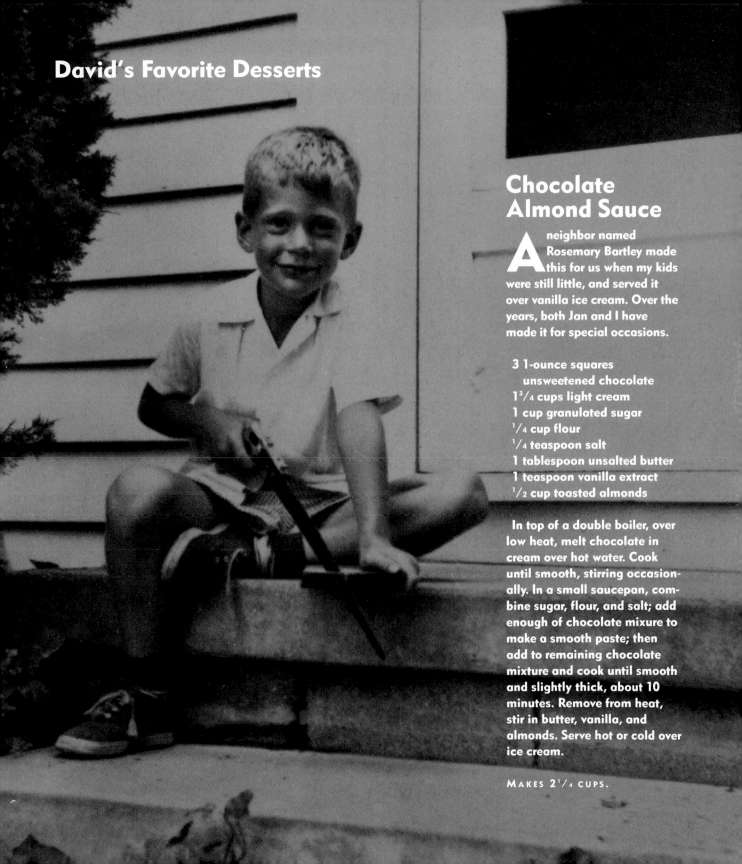

Chocolate Almond Sauce

A neighbor named Rosemary Bartley made this for us when my kids were still little, and served it over vanilla ice cream. Over the years, both Jan and I have made it for special occasions.

3 1-ounce squares
   unsweetened chocolate
$1^3/_4$ cups light cream
1 cup granulated sugar
$^1/_4$ cup flour
$^1/_4$ teaspoon salt
1 tablespoon unsalted butter
1 teaspoon vanilla extract
$^1/_2$ cup toasted almonds

In top of a double boiler, over low heat, melt chocolate in cream over hot water. Cook until smooth, stirring occasionally. In a small saucepan, combine sugar, flour, and salt; add enough of chocolate mixure to make a smooth paste; then add to remaining chocolate mixture and cook until smooth and slightly thick, about 10 minutes. Remove from heat, stir in butter, vanilla, and almonds. Serve hot or cold over ice cream.

MAKES $2^1/_4$ CUPS.

CHOCOLATE CHIFFON PIE

David's Favorite Desserts

David always preferred this pie to cake on his birthday, so I would put candles on his chocolate chiffon pie. I have included a recipe for the crust, but a 9-inch store-bought graham cracker crust is also good.

CRUST
1 cup vanilla cookie crumbs
½ cup finely chopped pecans or walnuts
2 tablespoons granulated sugar
3 tablespoons unsalted butter, melted

In a small bowl, combine ingredients. Spread over bottom and sides of 9-inch pie pan and pat down firmly. Chill.

FILLING
1 envelope unflavored gelatin
¼ cup cold water
2 squares unsweetened chocolate
1 cup milk
⅛ teaspoon salt
3 eggs, separated
½ cup granulated sugar
1 teaspoon vanilla extract
Whipped cream for topping

In a small bowl, soften gelatin in cold water. In top of double boiler, over low heat, combine chocolate and milk. Stir over boiling water until chocolate melts. Beat until smooth, then stir in gelatin. Add salt to egg yolks; beat until thick. Gradually beat in ¼ cup sugar. Slowly add to chocolate mixture, stirring until blended. Return over boiling water, cooking until slightly thickened. Chill. In a small bowl, beat egg whites until stiff. Gradually beat in remaining ¼ cup sugar. Add vanilla to chocolate mixture and fold in whites. Pour into crumb-lined pan. Chill. Serve with whipped cream.

OLD-FASHIONED SUGAR CREAM PIE

I concocted this recipe by taking the best ingredients and suggestions from three different sugar cream pie recipes. I've had it for years and the whole family likes it.

1 8-inch unbaked pie shell (see page 150)
½ cup granulated sugar
½ cup packed brown sugar
½ cup flour
Dash of salt
2 cups heavy cream
Freshly grated nutmeg

In a small bowl, mix sugars, flour, and salt. Gradually stir in heavy cream. Pour into pie shell and sprinkle with grated nutmeg. Bake at 400 degrees for 15 minutes. Reduce heat to 350 degrees, bake for 20–25 minutes longer.

Note: Center of pie will be slightly runny when done.

SOUR CHERRY PIE

Since I can't send the chocolate chiffon pie overnight to David, this is the dessert I usually send to him for his birthday—or if I'm just thinking about him. First, I freeze the pie, wrap it tightly in Saran Wrap, wrap it again in bubble wrap, and fold newspaper around it. There's a box store nearby that sells boxes that just about fit the pie, so I pack it in one of those and send it overnight express. Once, when David was still at NBC, I was watching his show and I saw him pull out the cherry pie I had sent to him a couple of days earlier for his birthday. There was a big wedge cut out of it and a big bolt lying in the pan. He told millions of people that I had baked a stove bolt in his pie. Oh, David, I did not!

Pie dough for 2-crust pie (see page 150)
1 cup granulated sugar
¼ cup flour
4 cups sour cherries
Dash salt
Unsalted butter

In bottom crust, mix and add ¼ cup sugar and 2 tablespoons flour. Distribute evenly. Add cherries, remaining sugar, and flour. Sprinkle a dash of salt over all. Top with butter cut into pieces. Cover with top crust, turn edges under the bottom crust, and crimp to seal. Cut slits in top of crust. Sprinkle with a little sugar. Bake in 450-degree oven for 20 minutes. Finish baking at 350 degrees for about 30 minutes. To prevent crust from becoming too dark, cover the edges with foil when you reduce oven temperature.

David's Favorite Desserts

STRAWBERRY PIE

Two years ago when David came to town for the Indianapolis 500, he called and said he was going to the Steak 'n' Shake for burgers. We were grilling burgers at my house and I suggested that he come eat with us, but he said that he wanted Steak 'n Shake and would come here later. Hans and I had picked strawberries that day, so I quickly put together this strawberry pie. If David wouldn't have homemade burgers, at least he could have a homemade dessert. He loved it!

1 9-inch baked pie shell (see page 150)
1½ pints fresh strawberries, washed and hulled

GLAZE
½ cup granulated sugar
2 tablespoons cornstarch
¾ cup orange juice
½ teaspoon red food coloring
Whipped cream, for topping

Mix sugar and cornstarch, then add orange juice and food coloring. Cook until clear. Add strawberries to glaze and pour mixture into pie shell. Serve with whipped cream.

THE LATE SHOW HOUSE SPECIALS

These recipes also came from members of the *Late Show* staff. I thought you might get a kick out of reading them.

HAL GURNEE'S PLANKED CODFISH

Hal Gurnee worked as a director and supervisor for David from 1980, when David was doing his morning show, until 1995, when he retired. Mr. Gurnee got this recipe from his grandfather, who was a boat captain. They would catch the fish from Lake Superior, then cook it on the plank right there on the boat.

> *A clean hardwood plank, well oiled and seasoned*
> *Pastry bag and tip*
> *3 pounds codfish fillets*
> *4 tablespoons unsalted butter, melted*
> *1 egg yolk*
> *3 cups mashed potatoes*
> *Lemon slices*
> *Salt and pepper to taste*

Preheat oven to 400 degrees. Pile the codfish fillets in the center of the oiled hardwood plank, leaving a 3- to 4-inch border. Brush the fish with some of the melted butter. Set the plank directly on the rack in the oven. Bake 20–25 minutes, until the fish starts to brown. Stir the egg yolk into the mashed potoates. Fill the pastry bag with the potato mixture. Remove plank from oven and pipe a wall of potatoes around the fish. Drizzle the fish with the remaining melted butter. Place under the broiler until the potatoes begin to brown. Remove the plank from the oven and garnish with lemon slices to serve.

MAKES 6 SERVINGS.

Gracie's Dinner

I was very surprised when I got a recipe for homemade dog food, then I thought, hey, that's kind of neat. This dog dish is from "The Late Show's" Pet/Human Tricks coordinator, Susan Hall Sheehan, who has been with David since 1983. She screens all the audition videotapes that people send in, and also orders office supplies. She makes this homemade dog food for her Boston terrier, Gracie.

$^2/_3$ your pet's favorite dry food to:
$^1/_3$ leftovers or wet pet food
1 squirt tap water

Stir ingredients together and zap in microwave 10-20 seconds or until warm. (If no microwave use hot tap water.) Stir once more before serving and be sure it's not too hot.

Susan says: "Gracie's never had a choice, but consistently eats dog chow from the ten-pound bag, and she will chow down even the most questionable leftovers as long as meat is involved. You can subsitute gravy for tap water but don't do anything you're not prepared to do for every remaining meal of that pet's life! This recipe may also work for cats if you substitute water from a can of tuna fish for tap water."

Good ol' Tippy, my childhood pet and playmate.

DOG JACKS

From Steve O'Donnell, a writer for *The Late Show*. He has been writing for David since 1982, and came up with the idea for the show's famous "Top Ten List" and Big Ass Ham. As you can see from this recipe, Steve has a real sense of humor so I'm not sure he's serious about this recipe. Even though a waffle iron is used, he calls them dog jacks, after the flapjack. I guess he's better at comedy than cooking.

> *1 package hot dogs*
> *2 eggs*
> *Blender*
> *Waffle iron*

Steve says: "Drop the hot dogs into the blender. Add a couple raw eggs so the mixture will have some cohesion. Liquefy, or as close as you can get. Pour the 'meat batter' onto a hot waffle iron and start cranking out your delicious Dog Jacks! They're part hot dog, part flapjack—and completely wonderful! The Letterman family seems to love their fried baloney—and this recipe is my loving tribute to them."

DOROTHY SAYS:

LIVING WITH PRESSURE

When I was a little girl, my mother cooked her potatoes on a coal stove, but when I was in high school, she introduced me to the joys of pressure cooking. Since the 1950s, when my kids were young and I got a pressure cooker of my own, I've cooked just about everything in it. Potatoes can be done in 10 minutes and green beans come out tender and flavorful (see page 121). Pressure cookers were very popular for a while, then people stopped using them, maybe because of their tendency to blow food to the ceiling if not used properly. In fact, when I replaced mine about five years ago, my hardware store had to order one because they weren't kept in stock. Lately there's been a pressure cooker revival, and the new ones are safer to use. (I see they're even sold at Williams-Sonoma now.) I pop popcorn in mine (without the pressure top on), because the shape of the pot pops the kernels very nicely. It's good for other foods, too, because the goodness and nutrients don't get cooked out. And it works so fast, *you* won't get cooked out, either.

A CURE FOR CRICKETS

One hedge apple (Osage orange) in the garage and one in the basement will discourage crickets when they become a nuisance in the fall. The Osage orange is an ornamental moraceous tree with fruit resembling an orange with warts. They're native to Arkansas, and thrive in surrounding areas. They also grow in Indiana. The tree is often used to form decorative hedges or fence rows, hence the more common name, hedge apples.

HOMEMADE BAKING POWDER

I usually buy a can of baking powder, which lasts a long time, but it's great to know I can also make it from scratch.

SIFT TOGETHER:
2 tablespoons cream of tartar
1 tablespoon cornstarch
1 tablespoon baking soda

Combine and store in an airtight container. One teaspoon of this baking powder is equal to 1 teaspoon of the store-bought kind.

DOUBLE OR NOTHING

Soon after I got my first chest-type freezer in 1983, Hans and I were picking asparagus in southern Indianapolis. The gal overseeing the asparagus patch told me to double-bag the vegetables we planned to freeze in order to avoid freezer burn, which dries out the vegetables. Double-bagging also eliminates freezer odor.

Homemade Window Cleaner

I swear by this window cleaner. Unlike so many of the store-bought varieties, it doesn't leave streaks. My friend Pat Foster suggested this recipe, which works beautifully.

1 gallon distilled water, divided
1 cup white vinegar, divided
1 cup isopropyl alcohol (available at drugstores), divided
Dishwashing liquid

Divide water into 2 $1/2$-gallon containers. Using a funnel, add equal amounts of vinegar, alcohol, and 1 squirt of detergent to each container. Can be transferred to small spray containers as needed.

Look! No streaks!

AFTERWORD

I've really had so much fun preparing this book. Going through my own recipes and jotting down stories about my family brought back many, many memories—some of them sad and touching, some of them funny. Looking back at my vegetable dishes, I recalled a time when Joe and I took Jan and David with us to a florist retailers convention. While Joe and I were attending a banquet, the kids ordered room service and their meal included asparagus. Well, David never liked asparagus, so he opened the hotel window and pitched it out. Luckily, no one was speared by falling asparagus. It reminded me of him dropping watermelons off rooftops on his television show. I guess some things never change.